HANDWRITING ANALYSIS
A COMMON SENSE GUIDE

JUDY INMAN

ILLUSTRATIONS BY KIP HEATLEY

HANDWRITING ANALYSIS
A Common Sense Guide

First Edition, December 1995
Humphrey Printing Company, Wichita Falls, Texas

Dedicated to my sister
BETTY JANKO
whose courage and optimism inspire
all who are fortunate to know and love her.

Some handwriting samples
have been reduced
in the interest of space.

Analyses given are excerpts
utilized to emphasize certain characteristics,
and no derogatory remarks are intentional
on the part of the author.

Contents

Acknowledgments

My sincere appreciation and "hats off"
to:

Ellen Magnis, whose patience, creative
talents and professional editing skills
made this book a reality,

Kathy Henscheid, for her enthusiastic
endeavors in gathering many of the outstanding handwriting samples
seen in this book,

Jim Inman, my husband of twenty-one years, for his enduring love
and constant support, in addition to his computer wizardry which
came to my rescue on a daily basis,

Alice Dohm, Shannon Inman, Summer Inman, Susan Blake, Flossie
Schoppa, and Eva Jane Haverkamp, for their special contributions,

Nadya Olyanova, a pioneer in the field of graphology, for her kindness to me as a young student; her amazing insight has always in-
spired me,

Kip Heatley, whose wonderful illustrations add a touch of humor to
these pages, and

All those whose personal handwriting appears in this book, for their
understanding in this endeavor.

Preface

As a kid, I was always the last one in a crowd to understand the punch line of a joke. "Somebody draw Judy a picture!" was a comment often made, at my expense. It's not that I wasn't smart; I was an honor student in school. I was always just a very analytical person who needed a logical, step by step explanation about something before it really made sense to me.

I was twenty years old when I read my first book on handwriting analysis, quite by mistake I might add. In a hurry one day, I picked up the wrong book in a department store, thinking it was a book about Egyptian hieroglyphics. I remember how disappointed I was later that night when I discovered my error and began to read about something called *graphology*. The more I read, the more fascinated I became with the idea. It was such a new and exciting revelation to me that I could hardly wait to analyze everyone I knew.

My enthusiasm went haywire! No one escaped my scrutiny. I analyzed the handwriting of all my family, friends and neighbors. When I finally exhausted every willing participant, I decided to experiment with my new found interest at work.

At the time I was a personnel counselor for a small employment agency. It was an ideal proving ground for my graphological pursuits. The owner of the agency expressed her reservations to me about the whole matter, but I was determined to test the waters. The results were amazing! A handwritten employment application suddenly revealed much more to me than just routine information. Even before checking out his references, I felt I had a real understanding about the applicant's true character.

I was able to detect basic personality traits that revealed whether he would be a good-natured cooperative employee, or an ill-tempered bothersome troublemaker.

In addition, I could quickly determine whether he was better suited for a people-oriented job in public relations, sales or management, or happier working alone in a more isolated environment. The answers were all there in his handwriting.

It wasn't long until my placements began to skyrocket! My success in the business was not only monetarily rewarding, but it gave me a tremendous amount of personal satisfaction as well. Even my employer was so impressed that she requested I teach the other counselors "my special ability."

That ability has been a major part of my daily life now for thirty-three years and has literally become second nature to me. I continue to analyze every scrap of writing within my reach. I enjoy teaching classes on graphology and giving programs to schools, clubs and various organizations. And no matter where I go or who I meet, it seems almost everyone I talk to is interested in handwriting analysis. The mere mention of the fact that I am a graphologist invites a wide variety of interesting responses.

The more skeptical disbeliever often retorts, "I'd hate for you to see my hen scratching! You might tell me I'm an axe murderer!" Then there are those who think handwriting analysis is something akin to fortune telling, and ask me for an instant "reading." I am still surprised to find that a lot of people associate graphology with the occult and assume it is related to a psychic or supernatural phenomenon.

But generally, most people recognize its true merit, as handwriting analysis today is widely accepted all over the world. It has without question, earned a respected place in a number of fields, including psychology, vocational guidance, and criminology.

Its infinite value in the realm of human relationships has yet to be fully appreciated, though it adds invaluable perspective into the developing personalities of children and intimate relationships between couples.

Perhaps its most significant role however, lies in the area of self-awareness. For handwriting analysis offers each individual the ability to better understand, and even change his own personality.

As a lifetime subscriber to the practice, I can highly recommend it! Nothing else has given me such unfailing insight into my own human nature or provided me with such real understanding of my fellow human beings.

Over the years, I have wanted to write a book on graphology, using a simpler, easier approach to an often complicated subject. I am hopeful this book will offer a basic, down-to-earth method for those of you, like myself, who may sometimes need a step by step explanation of how something really works.

Almost anyone can learn to analyze handwriting; you don't have to be a genius. The only requirements you really need are: a fair understanding of human nature, patience, determination, a little intuition, and a lot of common sense!

Introduction

Because no two people possess the same, identical handwriting, each individual creates a unique personality with every stroke he writes. Dictated by the mind, the hand draws a mirrored image of the writer's true fundamental character.

How you feel emotionally, mentally, and physically will determine how you write on any given day. Illness, temporary changes in mood, or any number of problems may affect your handwriting. If you are feeling frazzled or really "out of kilter," your handwriting may actually look as if it belonged to some-one else altogether. It all boils down to how you feel. But even throughout life's crises however, your basic personality traits will still surface in your handwriting.

It will reveal your ambitions in life and what strengths you possess to help you achieve your ambitions. Handwriting which contains *positive* signs of confidence, discipline, good judgment, and foresight reveals a well-adjusted person who is able to cope with the challenges of day to day living.

As revealing as handwriting is, there are a few things it does not reveal. For instance, it does not automatically deter-mine the writer's sex. Since men and women are comprised of both masculine and feminine characteristics, it is best to know the writer's sex before beginning an analysis.

Another factor handwriting cannot detect is age, for maturity is not always measured in terms of chronological years. Traditional text-book formations taught to the school-age child (large, rounded let-ters with initial lead-in strokes) are often seen in the handwriting of adults of all ages. You can be certain that something of the child still exists in those personalities, regardless of the age.

In like fashion, the child who seems older than his years will break away from traditional formations of textbook handwriting. His own independence will be most noticeable in the elimination of initial strokes on small letters. (See Chapter 1 for detailed indications.)

In the following examples, the age element is questionable, as both handwritings contain many of the same characteristics.

This is the handwriting of a thirteen year old girl who shows many signs of early maturity.

> School is okay. But she had
> problems with math, as always.
> I'm looking forward to
> Christmas, are you?
>
> *melissa Knapp*

Melissa - Age 13

This independent young lady shows a good deal of confidence and self-discipline in her handwriting. Her emotional, intuitive nature spurs her altruistic need to help others. Signs of good judgment are already beginning to emerge in her script.

Her reserved demeanor allows her to stand back and form opinions before allowing others too close. She is very practical, enjoys doing "fun" things and shows a good sense of humor.

Her signature expresses her cheerful, optimistic approach to life. She has a high energy level. (Melissa is an advanced student in school, serves on the student council, and is active in sports. She enjoys reading, writing stories, and is involved in a variety of community projects. Her long-range goals center around education.)

Major Emphasis: Heavy pen pressure, vertical slant, large size, firm centered/wavy/bowed/T bars, wavy i dots, large capitals, small open a/o, round/legible letters, connected/disconnected writing, wide word spacing, middle zone focus, rising baseline.

In comparison, this forty-eight year old man still retains many of the childlike qualities seen in the previous sample.

> My dear Judy
>   Your letter was received
> by way of William Hart. Since
> I have never had my handwritting
> analized before – I shall send
> this note along in hopes that it
> might help you with your book.
>   Sincerely.
>   Thomas A. Price

T.A. Price - Age 48

This gentle sample of handwriting displays a large measure of naivete', but it possesses genuine warmth, generosity, and true empathy for others. He is quite open and honest. His determined, practical attitudes enhance his logical thinking.

His strong feelings for order and harmony are essential traits of his artistic nature. (Thomas A. Price is a well-known sculptor of modern art forms. His work for many years has made a strong statement against the nuclear destruction of mankind.)

Major Emphasis: Medium pen pressure, right slant, large size, initial strokes, open small a, clear legible formations, firmly centered/star-shaped T bars, middle zone focus, elimination of loops on small h, connected writing with disconnections in the word "handwriting," thick shaded pen strokes, even rhythm and steady base line.

Another indication handwriting cannot determine is a writer's occupation although individual characteristics will reveal a particular aptitude for certain types of work. (See Chapter 6.) Many people work in jobs for which they are unsuited. Employment opportunities, lack of education, and financial difficulties are major stumbling blocks in this area. Personal satisfaction in the workplace often takes a backseat to the stark reality of a regular paycheck.

Even under the best of circumstances, many people continue to feel disillusioned and unfulfilled in their choice of vocation. The following is a prime example of a woman who is unsuited for her current line of work in the office of a law firm. Although she earns a substantial wage for her long hours, she is dissatisfied and wants to make a drastic career change.

Jana - Age 33

Jana's handwriting reveals her enthusiastic, optimistic, spontaneous approach to life. There is nothing "humdrum" about this vivacious personality. She is a confident, independent extrovert who rebels against anything remotely resembling conformity. She hates mundane, routine work and clearly wants to do something *different*.

Her common sense sometimes falls by the wayside, and where her emotions are involved, she is quite generous. She is physically active and has a warm, sensuous nature. A hint of secretiveness is evident which seems almost out of place in an otherwise straightforward handwriting. Even though she is extremely outspoken, she prefers to keep some things to herself. She is also highly imaginative and outrageously comical.

She would be more suited for a career in acting, sales (with travel), cruise directing, or public relations. Until she makes a career transition, however, she will no doubt fill her personal life with as much diversity as time will allow.

Major Emphasis: Medium/heavy pen pressure, right slant, very large size, rising baselines, extended finals, wavy T bar, legible/round letters, circle exclamation point, added smiling face doodle under signature, connected writing, large capitals, tangling lower zone, added pressure on long full lower loops, high i dot, high upper zone small l, small a in signature enclosed within capital J.

Aside from indeterminate factors of sex, age, or occupation, in most cases the graphologist is able to detect outstanding personality traits with a few lines of handwriting. Occasionally, the writer's signature may be omitted for reasons of privacy. Under these circumstances, an analysis can be made, but it does not always reveal a complete image of the character at hand.

In addition, any accessible information about the writer is helpful in providing a logical frame of reference. For instance, if the writer is suffering from depression, it would be useful to know in advance whether he had recently experienced the loss of a loved one. Or if the handwriting looks debilitated, being aware of a recent setback in the writer's health would explain breaks in his tremulous script.

In other words, use graphology as a sensible tool to provide a reasonable composite of the writer's present state of mind. If you possess a highly intuitive nature, you may be tempted to trust your instinctive "feelings" about a writer; however, beware of what you feel until you have studied the basic building blocks of graphology and have achieved some measure of practical success.

Chapter 1

Basic
Building
Blocks

Unless you have a photographic memory, trying to absorb the enormous amount of information available on the subject of graphology is next to impossible. It is much easier in the long run to grasp the logic behind the basic fundamentals.

In the first place, try to visualize handwriting as pure energy unleashed from the mind to the hand, and expressed through pen strokes on paper.

The *power* of that energy (both physical and emotional) is released in the depth of pressure wielded by the pen, and can be detected by feeling the impression on the underside of the paper. The deeper the imprint, the higher the energy level, and the greater the emotional intensity.

PEN PRESSURE

light   LIGHT pen pressure = faint impression on paper. Writer has a low energy level and may be ill. At best he is a very sensitive person.

medium   MEDIUM pen pressure = firm impression on paper. Writer has a healthy energy level and is emotionally balanced.

heavy   HEAVY pen pressure = deep impression on paper. Writer has a high energy level, and a strong emotional nature.

very heavy   VERY HEAVY pen pressure = impression bears hard into paper. Writer suffers emotional or physical frustration.

erratic   ERRATIC pen pressure = inconsistent light to heavy impression on paper. Writer has an erratic emotional nature or may be ill.

SHADED PEN STROKES: While evaluating pen pressure, the shade of the pen stroke will also be apparent. In like manner, the darker the pen stroke, the more sensual the writer. The artistic nature is also evident in the shade of the stroke (See page 17.)

SLANT

The direction of writing or slant, is an indicator of the writer's emotional expression. The further the writing leans to the right or left, the stronger the degree of expression, or lack of it.

RIGHT slant = writer expresses emotions freely, as he goes forward to meet the world.

VERTICAL slant = writer controls emotions, as he thinks, before reacting. He may appear aloof or reserved.

LEFT slant = writer does not express emotion freely, as he retreats back and away from the world.

VARYING slant = writer is suffering from conflicting emotions, which may be temporary. He may feel torn in opposing directions. (Varying T bars will corroborate conflicting emotions as well as other inconsistent factors.)

There are things in life worth
More than the sum of their
Parts. People constantly Suprise me
by reveiling a new aspect of them-
selves I had not noTed before.
Its fun !

For some time, Hans has been undecided as to his choice of profession. For the past five years he has been a registered massage therapist. He has recently enrolled in college and is majoring in Naturopathic medicine. He is a bright, ambitious young man with a keen interest in helping others. Varying slants accompany varying T bars and pen pressure in his handwriting to indicate uncertainty and conflicting emotions. (Future samples of handwriting may reveal more positive directions.)

SIZE

The size of writing is an indicator of the writer's view of things as well as his ability to concentrate. Large writing belongs to the extrovert who tends to generalize. Small writing belongs to the introvert. The smaller the writing, the greater the ability to concentrate.

The six most important words are "I admit I made a mistake."

Celine Dijkuris

MICROSCOPIC writing = Introverted writer possessing exceptional ability to concentrate. His energies are mentally focused, and he is often a recluse.

May Love, Peace and Joy be yours today, tomorrow and forever! My warmest Congratulations to you!!

SMALL writing = Introverted writer possessing strong ability to concentrate. He is modest, introspective, and prefers solitude.

You come by to see me sometime when she is here?

MEDIUM writing = Writer is realistic, and socially balanced. He is the doer rather than the thinker.

I loved him very

LARGE writing = Extroverted writer possessing great need for social interaction. His has diversified interests, and has difficulty concentrating.

Sue Yetter

VERY LARGE writing = Extroverted writer. The exhibitionist who wants to be noticed. He does everything on a grand scale.

ZONES

Handwriting is divided into three zones of expression. The writer's energies may be focused in a balanced manner in all three areas, or they may be exaggerated in a particular zone.

UPPER   MENTAL

MIDDLE   *high*   SOCIAL

LOWER   PHYSICAL

In writing which shows a balance between all three zones, the writer reveals an equal expression within his mental, social and physical make-up.

high

Where loops and stems reach high into the upper zone, the writer expresses great focus on idealism, imagination, and intellect.

high

Short upper loops and stems in the middle zone the writer expresses great focus on social and personal needs.

high

Where loops plunge down into the lower zone, the writer expresses great focus on physical, sexual, and material matters.

RHYTHM

The rhythm of handwriting is determined by the overall balance of combined features. Like music, writing contains repeated patterns and is released according to the writer's inner nature. Some music is slow and ponderous, while strong, quick rhythms produce livelier movement.

Harmonious rhythm is expressed by the writer's well-balanced, integrated qualities. Size, pen pressure, slant and spacing will be evenly distributed.

In handwriting where the rhythm is steadily and methodically released, the writer possesses a slow, controlled rhythm. He will deliberately slow down his writing to make certain his letters are formed according to his desires. Punctuation will appear firmly in place.

The speedy writer whose pen can hardly keep up with his mind expresses a fast paced rhythm. He will often leave out letters in haste, or slur word endings. A quick thinker, he is usually in a hurry to express his ideas. His T bars and i dots may fly enthusiastically to the right of the stem. He may also use printscript, an abbreviated form of handwriting, to quickly record the facts as he dashes along the mental path.

Disrupted rhythm reveals the writer's unpredictable moods. The overall tempo of the writing looks erratic and unbalanced. At best, the writer may be inconsistent.

T BARS

The way the writer crosses his Ts indicates the type of control his mind exacts. The writer's emotions and desires are governed by the amount of willpower he possesses. In general, the longer the T bar, the stronger the drive and determination. When other signs in the writer's script point to exaggeration, firmly crossed T bars will serve as a counterbalance. (Try tracing over the individual T bars to feel the energy it requires to make each formation.)

There are at least fifty different variations of T bars; some of the most common are:

long with hooks on beginning/end = tenacity. Writer has lots of nervous energy, with a strong need to keep active.

firmly centered bar = self-discipline, balance.

bowed through center = hand is controlled. Often appears in writing of surgeons or those using a steady hand in their work.

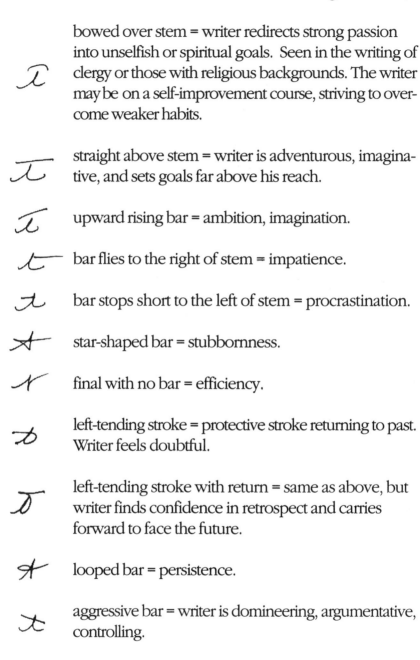

bowed over stem = writer redirects strong passion into unselfish or spiritual goals. Seen in the writing of clergy or those with religious backgrounds. The writer may be on a self-improvement course, striving to overcome weaker habits.

straight above stem = writer is adventurous, imaginative, and sets goals far above his reach.

upward rising bar = ambition, imagination.

bar flies to the right of stem = impatience.

bar stops short to the left of stem = procrastination.

star-shaped bar = stubbornness.

final with no bar = efficiency.

left-tending stroke = protective stroke returning to past. Writer feels doubtful.

left-tending stroke with return = same as above, but writer finds confidence in retrospect and carries forward to face the future.

looped bar = persistence.

aggressive bar = writer is domineering, argumentative, controlling.

tent-like stem = writer is stubborn and stands his ground.

single stroke stem = writer is pragmatic, efficient.

t̄   looped stem = hypersensitivity.

ᴇt̄   wavy bar = good sense of humor.

t̫   bowed under bar = writer takes line of least resistance and is often lazy.

Ⱦ   club-like bar = temper, sometimes violent.

t   light bar = writer lacks power to accomplish goals. He may be ill.

t t t   variety of T bars = writer is indecisive.

Joye's usual handwriting.

Joye's writing during a period of indecision.

i DOTS

The i dot will usually accompany a T bar with the same meaning although its main function is to determine the writer's memory retention. You may need a good magnifying glass to detect the shape of the dots, whether they are tent-like, wavy, or found somewhere down the page from the letter! These are the most commonly seen i dots.

i   i dot placed firmly over letter = writer is precise, has a good memory, and is very detail consciousness.

i   i dot placed high above letter = writer is imaginative.

i   i dot resembling tent = writer is critical.

i   i dot resembling wavy stroke = good sense of humor.

i   i dot placed to right of letter = impatience.

i   i dot placed to left of letter = procrastination.

i   i dot circled = artistic sign in handwriting with artistic leanings, or a bid for attention in other types of writing.

i   omission of i dots = writer may be absentminded or denying serious problem.

name.   single dot or period at end of signature = writer is asserting his power and will unlikely change his mind.

CAPITALS

Nora & Agnes came in last evening from a weeks visit to gives Phil

Sue Carter

The old fashioned capitals seen in this sample, were written by a Civil War widow. In 1870, she and her children traveled in a covered wagon from Mississippi to settle in Dexter, Texas. The capital A expresses her strong protectiveness. Also found in Abraham Lincoln's handwriting, it is indicative of the person who feels a definite paternal (or maternal) instinct. The old-fashioned M and N is usually seen in the same writing. More up-to-date versions of these letters will have the same meaning. The writer feels an instinctive need to protect others, especially those less fortunate. (Notice also the enclosed final stroke of the Carter signature, further confirming the protective characteristic.)

M N A A A

A B C F J K P R T

Printed capitals reveal simple tastes in the writer, as well as independence.

Debra Dill   D D

The open D reveals an open directness in the writer. It appears like an "open mouth". The writer may also find it difficult to keep confidences. The closed D reveals more caution in the writer. It appears like a "closed mouth". The writer may be secretive, especially if the next letter is enclosed within the capital. The added loop indicates flirtatiousness.

Unusual or unique-looking capital letters reveal inventiveness and originality. These are often seen in the writings of creative personalities including artists and writers.

The involved capital H is often seen in the handwriting of a manipulator or strategist. The writer manages one way or another to achieve his aims.

Inflated upper portion of capital L reveals generosity.

Inflated lower portion of capital L and inflated P reveals vanity.

Incurves on capital M and N (as well as incurves on any letter) reveal family pride.

When the second mound in a capital M is higher than the first, the writer feels a need to be in a position of authority to feel secure. If rounded, the writer's disposition will be gentle. If pointed, the writer will be more controlling.

THE CAPITAL I FORMATION

Aside from a writer's own signature, no other single indicator in handwriting is as revealing as the personal pronoun I.

This insistent capital letter is an adamant statement by the writer of his own personal self-worth. It can be either a very positive declaration that he is clearly confident or a negative indication of his low self-esteem.

Sometimes you will find a negative capital I in an otherwise strong, forceful handwriting, but more often it is seen in the modest unassuming script. Whenever it is seen, you can be certain that someone or something in the writer's life has caused him to think less of himself. In many cases this is due to an overbearing parent or spouse, and the writer needs reassurance to bolster his faltering ego.

Here are the most common capital I formations:

 Average I   = Writer is self-confident.

 Large I   = Writer is strongly self-confident. With accompanying right slant, heavy pen pressure, positive T bars, and wide line spacing, the writer shows management or leadership potential.

 Inflated I = In a large writing with additional strengths, reveals a strong self-image. In a writing with negative aspects, reveals vanity.

 Small I   = Writer has low self-esteem. May be too modest or underestimate his abilities.

Single stroke I = Writer is independent. Clear thinking and pragmatic, he is aware of his negative as well as positive attributes.

Printed I with serifs = Writer is extremely independent, self-motivated and does not look to others for support.

Right-tending I = Writer looks to others for approval and is too compliant.

Left-tending I = Writer is guarded, protective and pulls back to reflect before allowing too much intimacy.

Reverse I = Writer rebels against traditional rules and prefers to do things in his own way. (You may have to watch the writer to determine his left to right formation of this letter.)

Variety of I's = Writer may be inconsistent in his self-image, wavering day-to-day in his uncertainty.

Looped upper I = Often found in British writers and/ or those who are highly creative.

Lower case small i = Writer lacks confidence.

SMALL LETTERS

Small open a and o reveals generosity in the writer.

Small closed a and o reveals secretiveness in the writer.

Ink filled ovals reveal a warm sensuous nature.

Ovals or letters filled with heavy blobs of ink or dark smeary letters reveal extreme sensuality in the writer, who may be violent.

Open lip on small b reveals gullibility in the writer.

Tightly closed small b reveals good business sense in the writer.

Blunt ending stroke of d or t reveals a controlling, unyielding quality in the writer. He will feel the necessity to have the final word in an argument.

The Greek d and e reveals the writer's literary ability or the desire for it.

Looped d and t reveals the writer's sensitivity.

When two or more variations of the same letters appear in the same writing, it reveals versatility.

Small printed s, a, or r reveals talent in the writer, although it may not be used.

The letter g when made like the figure 8 reveals versatility in the writer. Often found in handwriting with literary talent, it often accompanies the Greek d and e. In any handwriting it points to the writer's adaptability.

The letters g and y, without a loop, resembling the figures 9 and 7, point to the writer's mathematical ability, as well as good judgment.

❖ ❖ ❖ ❖ ❖ ❖

UPPER LOOPS

Emotional expressiveness is revealed in the upper loops of handwriting. The average upper loop which reaches just above the middle zone reveals the writer's ability to express his emotions in a sensible manner.

Full, wide, upper loops reveal the writer who is emotionally expressive, idealistic, imaginative, sensitive, and often musically inclined. If too exaggerated, he may be unrealistic in his expectations.

Short upper loops reveal the writer's practical nature. Often the sign of an undeveloped intellect, these are seen in the writing of children and young adults.

Compressed upper loops reveal emotional repression in the writer.

Upper loops partially broken may reveal illness in the writer (usually heart problems).

Retraced upper strokes reveal the writer's inhibited thinking.

Elimination of upper loops reveals the writer's ability to think clearly without emotional hang-ups. (When consistent, it points to pragmatic thinking.)

LOWER LOOPS

Lower loops extending down into the lower zone reveal the writer's interest in material and sexual matters. Indications are varied according to the length and form of the loop as well as the writer's pen pressure in the lower zone. The deeper the pen pressure, the greater the writer's desire to gratify his senses.

long

Lower loops which are equal in size to upper loops, combined with medium pen pressure, reveal a healthy interest in material and sexual matters.

longer

Exaggerated lower loops combined with added heavy pressure in the lower zone, reveal the writer's ardent sexual and material interests. If very heavy pen pressure, it often reveals frustration due to lack of outlet. Medium/heavy or light pressure reveals the writer's sensuousness to music and rhythm. Usually the writer who makes such "wide" gestures in his handwriting will make "wide" displays of generosity towards others, as well.

longer

Short lower loops combined with medium pen pressure, reveal less interest in sexual or material concerns. Loops which do not complete through to the basic line often reveal unfulfilled needs.

long   longer

Short lower loops which appear tremulous, broken or jerky reveal health problems or illness in the writer, especially combined with light pen pressure.

long

Angular lower loops reveal stubbornness in the writer. If exaggerated, reveals the writer's attraction to the unusual.

long

The rightward turn on the downstroke of the g and y, instead of a lower loop, reveals altruism in the writer. (The loop made to the left of the downstroke will return to the self, while the rightward turn will indicate an unselfish need to give to others.)

longer

Cradle lower zone formation reveals emotional ties to parent.

❖ ❖ ❖ ❖ ❖ ❖

INITIAL STROKES

Initial strokes on small letters are always a sign of the writer's necessity to "hold on" to the past and reveal strong dependency ties. A child uses lead-in strokes to assist him in forming letters. The adult who continues to write initial strokes (with round letters) still possesses a childlike nature. On capital letters, the initial stroke indicates less self-assurance. Though he may appear confident, he is often uncertain.

The initial stroke has always reminded me of Tiny Tim leaning on his wooden crutch. It gives the child something to rest on while learning to form letters totally foreign to him. In time, with emotional and mental maturity, he will eliminate the unnecessary stroke.

END STROKES

Rising end strokes reveal the writer's enthusiastic, agreeable disposition. A social-oriented person, he gregariously reaches out to others.

Long extended end strokes reveal generosity as well as curiosity in the writer.

Abrupt, short end strokes reveal the writer's capacity to be blunt and curt.

End strokes which are flung downward like whips reveal a bad temper in the writer. Heavy end strokes denote cruelty and resentfulness.

The end stroke which turns leftward reveals the writer's protectiveness. Instead of going toward the future with confidence, he feels the need to pull back to the past for reassurance.

CONNECTED WRITING

please Know

The writer who connects his letters one to the other, is a logical person who needs a reason for everything. He mentally forms opinions and reaches conclusions in a systematic, orderly fashion. If the writing is completely connected and contains single downstrokes, the person does not use his good judgment. Instead he may fall into repetitive patterns in his life, unable to learn from experience.

DISCONNECTED WRITING

Donna and Toni
Mignon and   *Pam Thrasher*

The writer who disconnects his letters allows intuition to influence his conscious thinking. He forms opinions and draws conclusions from feeling and sensing. How intuitive the writer is will depend upon the frequency of his breaks between letters. A good balance between logic and intuition will surface in the majority of writings. (The letters will connect three or four at a time, and lift momentarily when a glimmer of inspiration flashes into the writer's thought process.) Signs of good judgment will allow the writer to quickly and accurately form opinions intuitively. When no signs of sound judgment are present in an intuitive writing, the person's emotions may lead him astray. The more disconnected the handwriting, the more creative the individual. Consistent breaks between letters will be seen in the writing of poets, writers, artists, musicians or anyone who is highly creative.

Close your eyes little boy
Close your eyes now and dream.
Dream of rainbows and baseball
And lots of icecream.
Dream of puppies and ponies
And days filled with joy,
Dream all of the things
That I wish you sweet boy -

Mary Kathryn Goll

Notice the frequency of breaks between letters in Mary Kathryn's poem. She is highly intuitive. Consistent signs of good judgment indicate her "hunches" are not apt to mislead her.

CONNECTED/DISCONNECTED STROKES

Strokes that connect letters together reveal the writer's ability to relate to other people. This includes disconnected printing and printscript.

Wavy garland strokes = writer is warm, receptive, sociable.

Arcade strokes = writer is protective, reserved, controlled.

Angular strokes = writer is unyielding, aggressive, analytical.

Threaded strokes = Writer is evasive or may not fully communicate his thoughts to others.

Printing = writer is very independent; shy about expressing feelings; often a loner

Printscript = writer is a quick thinker. He uses abbreviated form of printing and writing, stripping down to the essential facts.

AND IN THE END you WILL
LOOK BACK UPON IT ALL AND WONDER —

YES. you SHALL PONDER —

John's mostly all-caps printing and wide word spacing reveals his independent personality. Right slant, medium/heavy pen pressure, and some letter connections indicate strong emotions although he is shy about expressing them. A slightly bowed T bar (above the stem) in line 2, reveals his ability to channel strong passions into productive endeavors. The large capital J in his signature reveals his love of music and quick rhythms. The tightly closed small o and final evaporating n in his signature corroborates his secretiveness and evasiveness (John is a construction inspector. He also composes and writes music. Although he enjoys some social contact, he is basically a loner and prefers an independent lifestyle.)

❖ ❖ ❖ ❖ ❖ ❖

BASELINE

The baseline of handwriting reveals the writer's stamina in the long-range completion of his goals. He may plug steadily along, waver here and there, or rise and fall, very much according to his mood, at the time.

We love you all and

Straight baselines reveal the self-motivated writer who maintains steady control of his own directions in life. He will reach his goals in a reliable manner.

On all the confusion

Rigid baselines reveal the writer's need for control in his surroundings. (Other signs will corroborate this trait.)

My name is Autumn Murly

Vacillating baselines reveal the writer who is more easily influenced by outside circumstances. He is susceptible to whatever may come along, and adapts his directions accordingly.

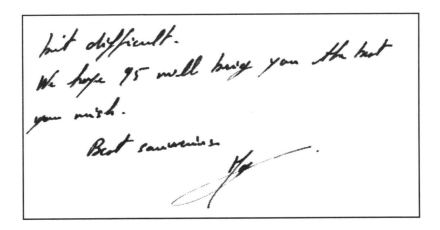

Rising baselines reveal an optimistic approach in the writer's outlook. Regardless of temporary setbacks, he will overcome problems with consistent enthusiasm.

Falling baselines reveal depression in the writer, which may be temporary. (You will need to examine several samples from the writer at periodic intervals.)

❖ ❖ ❖ ❖ ❖ ❖

SPACING

The distance a writer puts between himself and other people is indicated by the spacing between letters, words and lines.

Between Letters

Wide spacing between letters reveals the writer's ability to relate to others in a sociable manner. He is open-minded and tolerant.

Cramped or narrow spacing between letters reveals the writer's inability to relate to another person's viewpoint. He is often intolerant and narrow-minded.

Between Words

Wide spacing between words (wider than the size of the letter m) reveals the writer's need to distance himself from others.

Narrow spacing between words (less than the size of the letter m) reveals the writer's need for close relationships with others.

as much time as

Average spacing between words (approximately the size of the letter m) reveals the writer's ability to deal with others in a sensible manner.

She's doing good. I have finals in Wichita Falls, Texas in October.

Kim Nolan

Uneven spacing between words reveals the writer's inconsistent need for closeness. At times he may prefer more social contact, and other times prefer more privacy.

Between Lines

nice to hear from you. Hope every one in your family's doing well. Everyone's fine here. They send their love. Tell everybody "hello" from me. Hope to hear from you again soon.

Love,

JoAnna

Wide spacing between lines reveals the writer's desire to distance himself from others. Corroborating signs in this sample include wide word spacing as well as the vertical slant. JoAnna is a registered nurse. Basically a shy, reserved person, she is also kind and sympathetic. She is able to remain objective while making decisions (a positive asset for the nursing career).

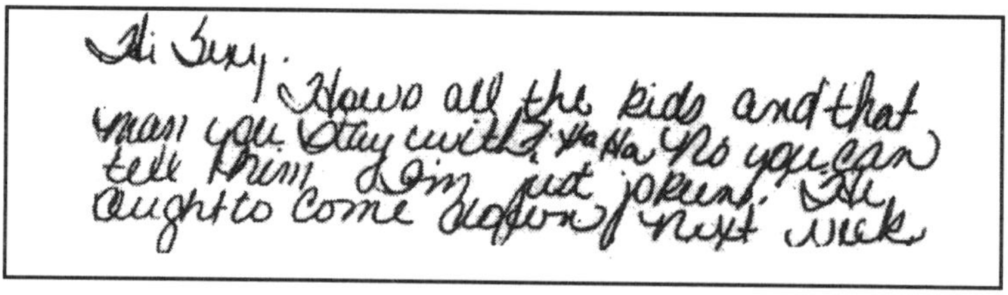

[handwritten note]

Narrow spacing between lines reveals the writer's desire for closeness and attention.

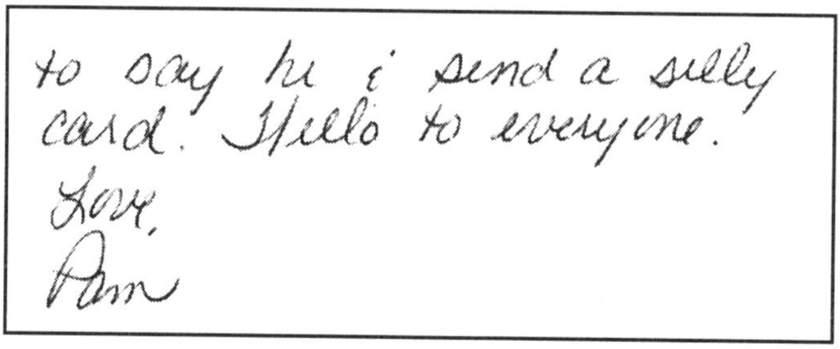

[handwritten note]

Average spacing between lines reveals the writer who possesses clear thinking and management ability (when combined with other signs). He is socially confident.

❖ ❖ ❖ ❖ ❖ ❖

MARGINS

There are varied opinions about the importance of the way a person sets his margins, and it is usually best to examine other factors of graphology, for corroborating signs.

A sense of economy is expressed by the writer who squeezes in every available inch of space on the paper. You can be sure he also crowds people and activities into his life in the same manner. Other corroborating signs will confirm this trait, including tangling lines and close word spacing. This is an actual letter written during the Depression. In an effort to economize, the recipient of this letter answered it by filling in between the lines and edges of the paper, before mailing it back to the original writer.

In this sample the writer leaves an even or framed margin, expressing his need for order and harmony in his surroundings. He is very organized and is something of a perfectionist.

> *Today is Monday, August 7th, 1995.*
> *The weather has been hot. Past*
> *week we had rain which helped*
> *break the heat. Fall will be*
> *here soon and then cooler weather*
> *will come.*
>   *Jenny Stromback*

This writer's left margin starts out even and grows wider as the writing fills the page. He is usually practical but may end up spending more than he intended. A generous person (emotionally as well as materialistically), he is usually in a hurry to get things done.

> *Did you know he is*
> *going on a long trip*
> *and won't be back*
> *until next month?*
> *I don't know how he*
> *plans to keep his job.*

The writer's left margin in this example grows narrower as the writing fills the page. The writer's practical nature may prevent him from being extravagant (a left-tending sign, the writer may retreat to the security of the past).

SIGNATURES

It's little wonder that we are so impressed with the signatures of well-known celebrities. A person's signature is his crowning glory. It is the image of himself that he presents to the world. The image may be exactly as he really is, or it may be a mask behind which the real personality resides.

Good luck,
Jim Brown

When the writer's signature is similar to the body of his handwriting, his public and private image are the same. When the writing is clearly legible, the writer desires to be understood.

When the writer's signature is illegible, he is expressing his need for privacy. Most probably, he does not care if he is understood by others. The body of his handwriting will reveal the true personality.

Good luck,
Jim Brown

When the writer's signature is larger than the body of his handwriting, the writer is aware of his importance and power over others. (Many public figures who maintain celebrity status, desiring to make a good impression, will write large signatures.)

Good luck,
Jim Brown

When the writer's signature is smaller than the body of his handwriting, he is expressing a less than confident opinion of himself.

Good luck,

Jim Brown

When the writer's signature is vertical and the body of his handwriting slants to the right, a barrier exists between himself and others. He appears aloof, but behind the public image may lie a demonstrative personality.

Jim Brown

When the writer's signature is underscored, the writer reinforces or asserts his personality. He may also be compensating for feelings of inadequacy, and this will be seen in the writer's capital I formations.

Judy as you can see, I can talk better than I write, THERE I GO AGAIN PRINTING: was one of four children, come from working class family, My brother who is older by two years could do no wrong, on the other hand myself could do no right

P.M. Pratt

Jake.

Jake has two signatures. His formal signature (P.M. Pratt) indicates his reserve and protectiveness (vertical slant, wide word spacing, enclosed final T stroke). The capital M, smaller than the other capitals, reveals a tendency to underestimate himself. The underscore in his informal signature is an added boost to his wavering self-esteem. The period after his name means he can say "no" with resolve. His handwriting displays several capital I formations. The upper looped capital I in lines 1 and 2, are typically British. The single stroke capital I in line 3, though a bit "short" reveals his independence. Rising baselines and wavy i dots reveal his optimism and jovial disposition. (Jake is an independent building contractor. A highly creative and talented individual, he is able to enthusiastically complete almost any project. His dry, British humor creates a fun-loving atmosphere.)

CELEBRITY SIGNATURES

Bill Cosby

Mario Andretti

Robin Williams

Clint Eastwood

Phil Donahue

Robert Goulet

January 30, 1995

Judy Inman
P.O. Box 492
Saint Jo, TX 76265-0492

Dear Judy,

I received your letter requesting a copy of my handwriting. Unfortunately, at this point I have a problem in providing you with a sample! I am right-handed. Last year I had surgery to repair a torn right rotator cuff -- and in the middle of the recovery from this -- I fell and fractured my right wrist. At the present time my writing skills are "out of commission." My "usual signature" does not look like what it normally does. I do hope you will understand, and I am honored that you would ask me.

Sincerely,

Mary Kay
Chairman Emeritus

MKA:jcd

Very little difference exists between Mary Kay's signature before *or* after her accident. This extraordinary woman has literally created an empire based on a foundation of love and kindness.

Her soft, round legible handwriting is unmistakably openhearted and straightforward. Connected writing and middle zone focus reveals her logical and practical nature. Rising finals express an enthusiastic, optimistic approach to life. Her shaded pen strokes and steady baseline reveals the personality of a self-motivating force that has made her one of the most famous entrepreneurs in the world.

CORROBORATING SIGNS:
THE ONE-TWO PUNCH

Many of the following signs will often appear in the same sample of handwriting and are corroborating signs of a particular trait. When one or more of these combinations is consistent, you can be reasonably sure the trait is a part of the personality make-up. I call it the one-two punch.

Some examples are:

◆Round letters + small open a and o = sympathy

◆Round letters + controlled rhythm = patience

◆T bars/right + i dots/right = impatience

◆T bars/left + i dots/left = procrastination

◆T bars/wavy + i dots/wavy = good sense of humor

◆T bars/rising upward + vertical slant = ambition

◆Even margins + T bars/above stem = perfectionism

◆Even word spacing + even line spacing + single downstrokes = organizational abilities

◆Wide upper/lower loops + small printed s = musical talent

◆Light pen pressure + T bar/bowed above stem = spiritual aims

◆Heavy pen pressure + right slant + long hooked T bar = strong driving force

◆Erratic pen pressure + erratic slant = writer is being pulled in too many directions; conflicting will

◆High upper zone loops/stems + high i dots = writer is imaginative (with addition of Greek e, d, or printed s and/or unusual looking capitals = creative intellect)

◆Long lower loops + tangling lines = confusion in writer's life.

Caution --- Warning Signs

Exercise caution when any of the following signs consistently appear in a sample of handwriting:

Falling base line and end strokes	DEPRESSION
Very illegible writing	NONCOM-MUNICATIVE
Extreme right slant	OBSESSIVE
Extreme left slant	WITHDRAWN
Extreme variation in letter size	INCONSISTENT BEHAVIOR
Smeary writing	EMOTIONAL INSTABILITY
Scratching out of words or letters	ANXIETY or STRESS
T bars which consistently fail to cross the stem	PROCRASTINATION; WEAK WILLPOWER
Club-like downslant T bar endings	TEMPER
Lines flung downward like whips	TEMPER

Imbalanced zones (depending on the zone which is out of proportion

EXAGGERATION

Excessive angular formations/sharp points on m's and n's

UNYIELDING; DEMANDING

Letters that grow larger at the end of a word

IMPETUOSITY

Excessively compressed upper loops

EMOTIONAL REPRESSION

Excessively compressed lower loops

SEXUAL REPRESSION

Cramped writing/letters formed too close together

NARROW-MINDED; INTOLERANT

Broken or ragged loops/tremulous writing

PHYSICAL ILLNESS

Strokes enclosing entire signature   SELF-INVOLVED

Excessive touching-up or tracing over

IMPROVEMENT;
PERFECTION; CLARITY

LEFT-HANDED WRITERS

Unless you know in advance whether a person is left-handed, you may not always be able to determine this factor. It is usually best to inquire about handedness when asking for information concerning the writer's sex, age and occupation. In general, the same rules of graphology will apply to both dextral (right-handed) and sinistral (left-handed) writing.

Some common indications will be evident in left-handed writing. Understanding the writer's handedness may prevent inaccurate assumptions. Awkward rhythm, erratic pen pressure and slant are common denominators in the sinistral handwriting. Uneven pressure often causes an imbalance on T bar crossings. For the sake of ease, the writer may cross T's from right to left, leaving a heavier stroke on the right side of the stem. Printing may often be more comfortable than writing, and unless the writer turns his paper to a different position, he will also produce a left leaning slant. The left-handed writer will develop a strong resolve at an early age in an attempt to adjust to a right-handed world. He is usually highly imaginative and creative.

Emmy award winner Michael Zaslow (alias, Roger Thorpe of The Guiding Light) is a natural "lefty."

In this letter, as in previous correspondence, Michael openly declares his dislike for his own penmanship. A general whirlwind of erratic signs envelops his script, which can be partially attributed to his left-handedness. His strong paternal instinct and need to protect those less fortunate are underlying characteristics in his handwriting. His ability to channel strong passions into lofty goals is one of his basic strengths. Headstrong and independent, he pursues his aims with determined fervor. He is open and outspoken in his beliefs. Basically a pragmatic, quick thinker, he also possesses good sound judgment. Creativity, imagination, idealism, talent and versatility are all outstanding attributes. A good sense of humor prevails along with an enthusiastic approach to life. (In reality, Michael is an entirely different character than the villain he portrays on television. He is an outspoken advocate for national health care and devotes a great deal of his time and energy in an unselfish effort to help *all* Americans.)

Special considerations: Left-handed writer.

Major Emphasis: Medium pen pressure, erratic slant, large size, double looped/bowed above stem/variable T bars, occasional heavy (right to left crossed) T bars, i dots to right of stem, wavy i dots, simple/printed/large capitals, modern/paternal capital A (more pronounced in other samples of writing), small printed s, open small a, round loopy small letters, angular m and n, single downstroke wide upper loops, no initial strokes, blunt finals, single downstroke capital I/small i, inconsistent letter size, looped small d, elimination of upper/lower loops, full wide lower loops, small cradle g, figure 8/small g, awkward rhythm, periodic disconnected writing, no margins, close/erratic word spacing, tangling lower zone, printscript, large letter endings.

Chapter 2

Twenty Questions: The Analysis

If you have read the previous chapter, you are probably wondering just how a handwriting analysis all fits together. There is so much to remember, and a lot of rules seem to apply in some types of handwritings and not in others.

It can really be confusing, especially if you've read several books on the subject and they all seem to contradict one another. One graphologist's method may differ from another, and interpretations may vary depending upon the person doing the analysis. The method you choose will inevitably be one that you feel the most comfortable with and makes the most sense to you. After all, the basic rules have not changed, just the names of the interpreters.

As a general guideline to these basic rules, I have compiled a list of twenty questions in this chapter to help you form simple, logical, and reliable conclusions.

NOTE: When gathering samples of handwriting in cases where you are not certain, ask the sex, age and occupation of the writer. Inquire about special considerations: whether the writer is left/right handed, whether any physical limitations (such as arthritis) exist, and whether he is undergoing any unusual emotional stress or depression at the time (brought on by illness, death of a loved one, divorce, etc.). Under such circumstances, you may need to examine several samples of writing over a period of time to determine if the indication is only a temporary condition.

Try to get at least a full page of spontaneous writing (on unlined paper), including the writer's usual signature. If you find a sample of writing that overwhelms your senses, put it aside until you have studied writing that is less complex. A good starting place is to choose the handwriting of a teacher or nurse; their writing is usually uncomplicated and displays traits of the "kinder, gentler" nature.

While answering the following questions, use a separate sheet of paper and refer back to Chapter 1, as needed, to refresh your memory.

1 What is your first impression of the writing; is it neat, messy, or confusing?

2 What, if anything, is outstanding about the writing; any unusual letters or formations?

3 Is the pen pressure light, medium, heavy, very heavy, or erratic?

4 Is the slant of the writing to the right, left, vertical, or varying?

5 Is the size of the writing microscopic, small, medium, large, or very large?

6 Into what zone does the energy flow: upper, middle, or lower; and is it proportionate?

7 Are the upper and lower loops long, full, short, or are loops eliminated?

8 Are the T bars long, short, high, star-shaped, bowed, wavy, or varying?

9 Do the i dots show humor, imagination, exactness, impatience, criticism, or are there omissions?

10 Are the small letters rounded, angular, open, closed, threaded or clear?

11 Do the capital letters reveal confidence, modesty, simplicity, or independence?

12 Is the basic line even or does it show optimism or depression?

13 Are the letters connected, disconnected or printed?

14 Are there any initial strokes and do end strokes rise up, extend outward, end sharply, or strike down below the basic line?

15 Is the rhythm of the writing consistent or irregular?

16 Do the margins look even; widen or narrow on the left or right?

17 Are letter, word and line spacings narrow, wide, or average?

18 Is the writing legible or illegible?

19 Is the signature larger, smaller, or the same size as the rest of the writing?

20 How often do the same signs appear in the writing; is it an occasional or consistent sign?

In forming conclusions about the writer, try to emphasize the overall picture, for example, look for indications which best reveal:

♦How the writer feels about himself:
    evident in capital letters, especially the capital I.

♦What image he projects to others:
    evident in the writer's signature.

♦How the writer reacts to others:
    evident in slant, letter connections, and middle zone.

♦If the writer achieves his goals:
    evident in T bars and baseline.

♦What kind of framework the writer functions in:
    evident in zoning.

♦What type of work the writer is best suited for:
    evident in all areas.

Before handing down the final verdict, here are a few common sense DO's and DON'Ts to remember:

-DO compare each independent factor and make determinations based on the entire writing.

-DON'T make snap judgments. For example, don't assume a single indication is a part of the writer's make up; look for corroborating signs to confirm the attribute.

-DO express reasonable opinions

-DON'T make absolute statements. For example, in expressing your opinion about the writer, be careful not to use words like "never" and "always." Be sure to make allowances for the variables in human nature. Most people are "never" "always" the same each and everyday, under each and every circumstance.

-DO express your findings with tact and diplomacy.

-DON'T criticize or judge too harshly. For example, most people don't mind being told they have the generosity of an Albert Schweitzer, but few enjoy being reminded of faults and shortcomings. And some people take a downright offensive attitude to an ego bashing! So use a little tact and diplomacy. To be on the safe side, I always check the writing to see how sensitive the writer is. If the writing contains small looped d's, I use more diplomacy in my choice of words. On the other hand, the writer who displays a single stroke capital I in his script can be more objective about the opinions you might express.

-DO accentuate the positive.

-DON'T dwell on the negative. For example, you will seldom find a handwriting which does not contain some positive attribute, even in the most negative case. Under such circumstances the writer needs to be reminded of the good side in his nature. Troubled personalities need hope, reassurance and above all, understanding. If you are confronted with a serious personality disorder, don't fall into the trap of trying to solve the writer's problems. Leave that to the professional.

When all is said and done and the written or verbal analysis is delivered, don't be too surprised to hear an occasional outburst of the writer's disagreement. "Well, I wrote that in a hurry" or "I don't usually write that way," are phrases often heard by the well-intentioned graphologist. Most people, however, will good-naturedly admit to a slight flaw in their character and think it's pretty amazing that you uncovered it.

Chapter 3

Early Indications

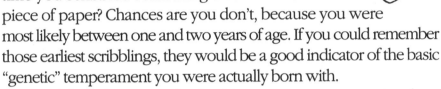

Do you remember the very first time you scribbled something on a piece of paper? Chances are you don't, because you were most likely between one and two years of age. If you could remember those earliest scribblings, they would be a good indicator of the basic "genetic" temperament you were actually born with.

Each baby begins to display his own temperament as early as two days after birth. While some babies lie calm and content in their cribs, other babies wave their arms and legs in restless activity; both indicate the type of personality they carried with them into this world. Each youngster will exhibit those same characteristics in early scribblings, drawings, and eventually his own individual style of hand-writing.

Before a child begins to draw anything resembling people or places around him, he scribbles lines, zig zags, or circles. The amount of space he uses on the page determines the amount of activity he requires. The more passive child uses only a small amount of space on the page, and requires a limited amount of activity.

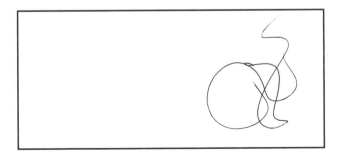

Circles, or round formations reveal a good natured, even tempered, and cooperative child.

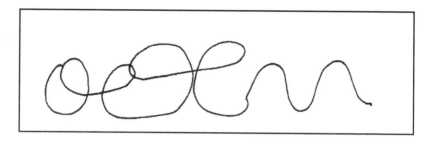

Zig zags or mazes of intertwining lines which fill up the entire page reveal the more aggressive, forceful youngster who demands greater activity.

Maria - Age 3

By the time a child is around four years of age he begins to draw things he most identifies with. In a loving, supportive environment, he might draw pictures depicting "happy" faces of parents, or brothers and sisters, to express his emotional security.

But the unhappy child who is experiencing some crucial problem often draws pictures expressing his inner turmoil. The following example is drawn by a young child who feels displaced by her divorced parents. She spends most of her time traveling between two families. Most noticeable is the overpowering size of the car, in proportion to the size of the house. The large areas of unused space reveal her feelings of isolation.

Youngsters who undergo traumatic changes often illustrate major differences in creative expression. Until recently Tommy drew colorless pictures of his mother's house where he resided. The drawings were always in black. Several months after his father received full custody of the child, color surfaced in Tommy's pictures, especially in the drawings of his father's home. Touches of orange, yellow, green and blue are emphasized in Santa's visit to his new home. Tommy's attitude has been transformed into a new, "brighter" outlook!

Tommy's new home after change in custody.

The examples are countless, depending upon the situation. The observant parent would be wise to pay close attention to his own child's special creative expression.

By the time a six year old attends school he is forced to abandon his natural expression, and the textbook method of handwriting is thrust upon him. He is taught to form initial strokes that lead into round letters. One by one he learns to connect letters together in a robot-like fashion. The whole process seems awkward to the average youngster and takes a few years for him to fully absorb.

Somewhere between nine and twelve years of age when the child begins to feel the unconscious habit of writing, his own individual personality begins to emerge in his script. Initial strokes begin to disappear. Round letters take on sharper edges, single strokes replace upper and lower loops, and breaks between letters sometimes occur. In addition those inclinations displayed in earlier scribblings resurface as an expression of the child's natural temperament.

When analyzing the handwriting of a child, special allowances should be made. The young child's writing may look inconsistent, uneven or messy. Words may be misspelled, scratched out, or rewritten in an attempt to make himself more clearly understood.

If possible a thorough handwriting analysis of the child's parents should first be considered to determine if any undue problems exist in the home environment. Children very often develop emotional problems from conflicts resulting from divorce or they may be suffering from any number of abusive situations. Each circumstance should be independently evaluated.

In chronological order, the following samples of children's handwriting reveal growing emotional and mental maturity, each at his own pace.

Melanie - Age 9.

This young girl's handwriting is slowly and deliberately produced. She is still uncomfortable with the formation of letters. Her self-confidence wavers now and then. Determination and aggressiveness are already apparent in her writing. An honest, practical approach to life plus a good sense of humor are outstanding traits in this youngster's developing personality. (Melanie is a third grade cheerleader. Computer games and animals are high on her list of favorite things.)

Major Emphasis: Medium pen pressure, right slant, medium size, middle zone focus, initial strokes, inconsistent capital I formations and letter forms, careful punctuation, downslant and wavy T bars, legible, connected writing.

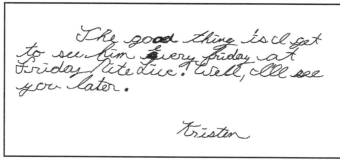

Kristen - Age 10.

Kristen's handwriting also reveals emotional dependency and signs of aggressiveness. Her strong determination, however, is intensified with a compulsive driving force. This confident young lady is always busy. Her nervous energy keeps her going on a nonstop basis. She can be almost relentless in her pursuits and quite stubborn in her convictions. She has a good sense of humor and a positive outlook. (Kristen's interests include anything that challenge her. She has a full calender of activities: performs with a drill team, is a talented artist and sculptor, recently landed a small role in a college play, and is even considering trying out for a local football team.)

Major Emphasis: Medium pen pressure, extreme right slant, medium size, downslant/wavy T bars/hooks, consistent wavy i dots, large capitals, tangling lines, initial strokes, extended/rising finals, inconsistent letter forms, maze of scribbles/letter corrections.

Brad - Age 11.

Brad is developing a confident personality early in life. A gentle, warm and friendly person, he is also very generous. His organizational skills are impressive for one so young, and he demonstrates a sharp eye for detail (characteristics certainly necessary for a career in architecture or archaeology). Logical connected script and a good sense of humor are representative of his father's handwriting on page 105. Certainly in this case, the apple does not fall very far from the tree.

Major Emphasis: Heavy pen pressure, varying slant, very large size, varying T bars, exact i dots, large capitals, legible/connected writing, wide letter spacing, inconsistent word spacing, wide line spacing, wavering baseline, rising finals, progressive elimination of initial strokes.

Amy - Age 12.

This adolescent's handwriting reveals a kind, gentle, personality. She is intensely emotional and very warmhearted. Though she appears friendly, she remains somewhat reserved, feels a need for recognition, and is often unsure of herself. Her strong aesthetic sense reinforces her artistic inclinations. (Amy is a typical preteen, faced with a multitude of conflicting emotions. She attends art classes that emphasize the creation of unusual artwork, pottery, and sculpture.)

Major Emphasis: Medium pen pressure, varying right/vertical slant, large size, signature/right angle, varying T bars, consistent initial strokes, circle i dots, thick shaded pen strokes, legible round letters, middle zone focus, undersized capital I, unusual A in signature.

Ben - Age 14.

Although this young man's handwriting still shows some emotional dependency, he is quickly maturing. There are numerous signs of confidence, independence, and self-discipline. A built-in reserve does not allow others too close, though once his trust has been won, he appears to be quite caring and compassionate. A strong paternal instinct exists in his writing, revealing an inherent need to protect those less fortunate. His desire for order and harmony is aesthetically defined. He has a high energy level and an athletic, competitive nature. (Ben is an outstanding student in school. In the past two years he has won 32 first place ribbons and medals in basketball and track competitions. Even though only fourteen years of age, he has already written to a number of colleges to inquire about his greatest ambition: playing professional basketball.)

Major Emphasis: Heavy pen pressure, vertical slant, large size, downslant/firm T bars, exact i dots, round/legible letters, elimination of initial strokes, large unadorned capitals, protective old-fashioned capital A, connected writing, signature/slight right slant, middle zone focus.

Lucas - Age 16.

Vacillating signs reveal a general uncertainty in this sixteen year old's restless handwriting. A lack of future goals often produces feelings of frustration. And though his sights have not yet been set, he certainly possesses strong potential.

Altruism is one of his finer qualities. He has a good sense of humor and an optimistic outlook. A quick logical thinker, he can be very practical. Once his mind is made up, he shows determination in completing a project. (Lucas is representative of many teens on the threshold of adult maturity. He has no definite plans for college or any career choice, as yet. At this stage in his life, he enjoys working on his truck and is interested in electronics.)

Major Emphasis: Medium pen pressure, right slant, large size, occasional initial strokes, inconsistent letter size, rising/ erratic baseline/word spacing/rhythm, middle zone focus, connected writing, variable T bars (long, wavy, bowed, hooked, down/upslant), wavy i dots, upper zone thrusts, altruistic small g, upper/lower compressed loops, small open o, sharp edges.

> My hobbies include cheerleading, country-n-western dancing, reading, listening to music, and having heart to heart talks with my good friends.
>
> Kim Urison

Kim - Age 18.

This bright young woman is beginning her college life with a good deal of maturity. She possesses sound practical judgment, talent, and on the whole, displays a steady, disciplined nature. Emotionally reserved, she thinks before reacting. But once attachments have been formed, she is quite loyal and caring. She exhibits strong ties to the past, and a need for closeness. Signs of a rebellious nature show her independent capacity for "doing things her own way". She is a streamlined intelligent thinker, who shows a good balance between her logical mind and her intuitive feelings. These positive attributes reveal her aptitude for any number of conventional careers, for which she would be most suited. (Kim seems much older than her young years. She has a wide range of interests, many of which she shares with her mother [who is her best friend]. Despite mixed feelings about leaving home, Kim has enrolled as a freshman at Texas A & M University. Her fall classes include biology, accounting, and math.)

Major Emphasis: Medium pen pressure, vertical slant, medium size, T bar variations, round small letters, printed simple capitals, consistent letter size, reverse capital I, consistent elimination of loops, steady base line, printscript, irregular word spacing, close line spacing, occasional initial stroke, left-tended loop in capital K, small printed s, middle zone focus, careful punctuation, occasional i dot to left/ahead, cradle lower zone small g, connected/disconnected writing, small open o, signature/same size/slight right angle.

Watching a child grow from dependent toddler to self-reliant adulthood, is one of life's most rewarding experiences. In a loving, reassuring environment, a child more than likely feels the freedom to verbally express his likes and dislikes. By encouraging his natural talents you can help him develop his own self-awareness and independence.

If your child is more withdrawn and develops an inability to openly communicate with others, looking carefully at his scribblings, drawings, and handwriting over the years will give you a clearer understanding of his inner thoughts and distant feelings. Your ability to understand, support, and encourage your child's individuality now will have a great bearing on who he may eventually become.

Chapter 4

Legendary Examples

Few celebrities are held in such high esteem with the public as the four major personalities whose handwriting appears in this chapter. Their words and actions, their tough, often outspoken, "no nonsense" attitudes, have endeared them to millions of people everywhere. They reflect the shining examples of honest, hard-driving, fearless Americans who get what they go after, against any and all adversity.

Common threads bind their handwritings together. They each possess an almost inexhaustible drive and determination. Their confident independent spirits seem to thrive on the unattainable, and they continually seek perfection. To be sure, their writing is often exaggerated, but there is nothing small about these larger than life characters. Each in his own endeavor has made a lasting impression on our culture and a real contribution to our way of life.

To most of us they remain heroes and we stand somewhat in awe of their dynamic personalities. Perhaps through their handwriting we can better understand the qualities that made each of them such extraordinary human beings.

Vince Lombardi

The physical pressure of Vince Lombardi's handwriting was equal to the power of his indomitable will. The force of his driving energy occasionally tore through the paper. Long, hooked T bars towering the upper zone proclaimed his high-reaching goals. His constant quest for perfection no doubt produced feelings of disappointment at times.

He was a man of good judgment and a logical thinker. He rarely trusted his intuition, as he felt more comfortable following a set structure of rules. An altruistic need to contribute something of value to others is an underlying factor in his handwriting; he obviously extended himself beyond normal limits to accomplish this end. Emotionally intense, he stood by his beliefs with firm resolve. Indeed he could say "no" and mean it. And though he was outspoken, he could also be very secretive and preferred to keep some things to himself.

Falling baselines and omission of i dots (in write, kind, and Vince) reveal denial of a problem too troubling for him to admit. Frustration is apparent in upper compressed loops. Perhaps the state of his health during this later period in his life was beginning to concern him. In any case, his determination was as strong as ever. This sample was written in late 1968. Lombardi died in September 1970.

He is not only remembered for his competitive spirit and outstanding coaching accomplishments but for his humanitarian efforts as well. His legendary personality continues to epitomize America's highest standard of excellence and perfection.

Major Emphasis: Very heavy/erratic pen pressure, right slant, very large size, long T bars/hooks reaching high into upper zone, even margins, correction of capital P in the word Please, overall good spacing, altruistic small g, whips in lower zone, added pressure on downstrokes in lower zone, compressed upper zone loops, inconsistent letter strokes/lower zone, inconsistent letter size, omission of punctuation, falling base lines, tightly closed small letters with additional loops encircled, looped small d, connected writing (exception in analyse [sic]), triangular shape small f in for, very large capitals, period after signature.

ROBERT WHITEHEAD and ROGER L. STEVENS

present

KATHARINE HEPBURN

KATHARINE HOUGHTON HEPBURN

II - 26 - 1977

Dear Judy Inman

> Your analysis makes me
want to understand handwriting better. I
sound fascinating. Maybe we write as we
would like to be. On the whole I think you
are amazingly accurate.

> One really sort of gets onto
one's self and yet one doesn't understand
oneself - very odd.

> You express yourself with great
clarity.

> It was fun.

> Thank you.

Katharine Hepburn

The handwriting of America's most honored actress overwhelms the graphological eye. Single adjectives hardly seem adequate to describe this astonishing personality.

Her unusual writing paints a confident self-portrait, expressing a brilliant creative intellect that is truly one-of-a-kind. She is staunchly independent, fiercely outspoken, and tenaciously determined. Her tireless energy is channeled into a rich fantasy world. But that does not prevent her from being sensible, for she is basically a pragmatic individual. Her logical, analytical mind is able to cut to the core of things, paring down unnecessary details. She has the added depth of intuitive perception, allowing her to "see" into people and situations, as well as the characters she so vividly portrays.

Her literary talent and appreciation for art is evident along with a strong aesthetic sense which expresses her need for order and harmony. She is the consummate perfectionist who sets goals far above the norm and expects to attain them. With such strength and stamina, one wonders how she could ever fail!

Quite secretive and evasive, she feels a strong need to distance herself from others, yet those close to her know the great generosity of her spirit.

(Ms. Hepburn has won 4 Academy Awards for her unforgettable performances. Her enigmatic personality, remarkable talent, and individualistic style continues to amaze a revering public.)

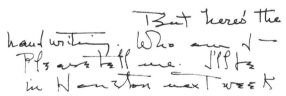

Major Emphasis: Medium size, vertical slant, medium pen pressure, open small a, long/hooked T bars, upper zone focus, high i dots, connected and disconnected writing, unusual/large/simple capitals, single stroke capital I, elimination of upper/lower loops, Greek e, printed s, blunt finals, threaded word endings, wide word spacing, even margins.

John Wayne

When you think of American heroes, John Wayne immediately comes to mind. In 150 films he usually portrayed the good guy who came to the rescue of the underdog. Even today, 16 years after his death, he remains the American ideal.

John's signature was an obvious attention-grabber, for he enjoyed playing center-stage. Always in the limelight, he strived to create a good impression; signs of secretiveness suggest he tried to maintain some measure of privacy in his personal life.

Enormous capitals and intertwining formations reveal the self-involvement of a gigantic character. The lower bulb of the capital L corroborates his vanity. Doing things on a regal scale was part of the private as well as the public image. He was physically energetic and very much the outdoorsman. A warm, intensely emotional person, he was also easygoing and somewhat childlike.

There are no T bars in this sample to gauge his drive, but we can clearly see his determination in connected letters and words. The lower looped y in Wayne reveals his lavish generosity and indicates his exaggerated sexual and material interests. Without a doubt, he possessed a tremendous passion for life, and he lived it to the fullest. (John Wayne died in 1979. His legendary film character lives on as the personification of the great American hero.)

Major Emphasis: Heavy pen pressure, right slant, very large size, lower zone focus, involved signature, tangling lines, connected letters and words, exaggerated capitals, large lower bulb/capital L, enclosed small letters within capitals, initial stroke on u, left-tending capital J, loopy formations, and rising baselines.

State of Texas
Office of the Governor
Austin, Texas 78711

ANN W. RICHARDS
GOVERNOR

August 10, 1993

Ms. Judy Inman
Route 1
P.O. Box 492
Saint Jo, Texas 76265

Dear Ms. Inman:

Thank you so much for the wonderful
cookbook. What a delightful idea for you
to share with your four granddaughters!
I know that Lillie and I will enjoy making
your recipes.

I appreciate your support and kind words.
Thank you for thinking of me.

Sincerely,

ANN W. RICHARDS
Governor

AWR/mi

I'd love to put my feet up & have tea but in all honesty, they don't find time on my calendar for F-U-N. Next year is election year and that even makes it worse! A.

Post Office Box 12428 Austin, Texas 78711 (512) 463-2000
Not Printed At State Expense

Ann Richards

Former Texas Governor Ann Richards expresses a charismatic personality through her handwriting. Immediately noticeable is her dynamic signature. An exaggerated capital A declares her power of authority. The open letter combined with legible writing reveals her honest, outspoken nature. She is direct and straightforward.

Her leadership qualifications are numerous. She has an ample supply of determination, good judgment, analytical ability and business expertise. Her common sense enables her to relate to others on a practical level.

Basically a "people" person, she is warm and receptive. The wavy extended final on her signature is an extension of her generous, fun-loving disposition. Lighthearted and spontaneously enthusiastic, she approaches life with an optimistic joie de vivre!

Major Emphasis: Medium pen pressure, shaded strokes, right slant, very large size, variety strong T bars/bowed/centered/wavy/upward rising, exact i dots, open/exaggerated capital A, larger/signature, connected writing, steady/rising baselines, tangling lines, middle zone focus, initial strokes, wavy/extended /rising/finals, small closed b, single downstrokes, angular m's and n's, legible writing.

Chapter 5

Life Crises

Case History #1: Betty Janko

On December 7, 1993, a lone gunman walked aboard a Long Island, New York commuter train and shot nineteen innocent by-standers. Amy Federici, a beautiful twenty-seven year old woman, was one of those victims. For nearly five days she remained on a life support system. Amy's parents, Jake and Arlene Locicero, and her sister Carrie, made the difficult decision to remove Amy from life support. They compassionately donated her organs to the nation-wide Organ Donor Program. Amy's heart, liver, and one kidney were donated to three New York area recipients. Betty Janko, a fifty year old woman in Dallas, Texas, received Amy's second kidney.

Betty had been on a kidney dialysis machine for five years. For nearly two years she had been on the waiting list for a transplant. Her physical vitality was growing weaker with each passing day. Normal activities had become almost impossible for her to achieve. Chewing just a few bites of food was an exhausting effort.

Throughout the waiting period, however, Betty maintained her usual positive outlook and never gave up hope. Her handwriting be-fore the transplant shows a deterioration of letter formations as her energy level diminished. T bars which were once strong, look faint and barely touch the paper. Her baseline and finals remain steady, showing her continued efforts to "hold on" with confidence.

Betty - Before transplant.

A year after the transplant, she wrote the following sample of writing. Notice the darker pen pressure. Heavier pressure on T bars reveals her new vitality and displays a normal energy level.

This is a sample of my handwriting now that I have a good kidney.   Betty J. Janke

Betty - After transplant.

Betty can now do anything she chooses. She walks a mile every day, serves on the Board of Directors of the National Kidney Foundation-Dallas Chapter, is a volunteer for Share Foundation, and works full time in the accounting department of a large cable company. She has also written a cookbook especially designed for healthy lifestyles (Eat Healthy Eat Well).

Her handwriting reveals an idealistic, cheerful approach to life. The entire script is balanced with signs of independence, good judgment, intuition, self-confidence, and determination. She is very logical, practical and unpretentious. Her organizational skills and math aptitude add to her savvy business sense. She has good powers of concentration, and her analytical mind loves a challenge. Because of the detail work involved, she also enjoys sewing and creating cross-stitch projects.

At Christmas last year, Betty sent the Lociceros a cross-stitch sampler that she personally made for their family. It read:

xxxxxxxxxxxxxxxxxxxxxxx
Life isn't measured
By the years you live,
But by the deeds you do
And the joy you give.
xxxxxxxxxxxxxxxxxxxxxx

In January, Betty will be flying to New York to meet the Lociceros, as well as the other organ recipients, for the first time. The courage and compassion exhibited by all those involved in this miraculous story has touched the hearts of Americans everywhere.

Case History #2:
Flossie Schoppa

A tornado nearly a mile wide ripped a path of destruction throughout the Red River Valley area of north Texas and southern Oklahoma, on Sunday, May 7, 1995. Several deaths were reported as well as countless injuries. Many families were left homeless, and businesses were devastated.

Fortunately, Flossie Schoppa was not at home when the tornado completely destroyed her residence near Bulcher, Texas. Upon arriving at the scene, she found her home and her husband's business leveled to the ground. Automobiles, trucks, and tractors were cast around in twisted forms. Everything she owned was scattered in bits and pieces over several miles of farmland.

Almost immediately neighbors, friends, and compassionate citizens from neighboring communities all joined together to give aid to the Schoppa family. Someone donated a trailer for temporary living quarters, and an abundance of food and clothing continually poured into the area.

In the aftermath, Flossie seemed in fairly good spirits. But as time passed, the reality of what she had lost finally began to dawn on her.

March - sign in sheets

Flossie - Before tornado.

Her handwriting shows a strong extroverted personality before the incident. She is gregarious by nature, very generous, and exhibits childlike enthusiasm. (She was a schoolteacher for many years and a District Administrative Aide to a Texas State Representative. Her busy schedule also included a wide variety of community projects and taking care of her grandchildren.)

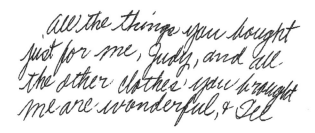

Flossie - One month after tornado.

Emotional disorder is seen in this sample. Notice the base line rising up and down in the first line. Depression is evident in the falling base line in the word "brought," while erratic pen pressure calls attention to her periodic mood changes.

Flossie - Four months after tornado.

Flossie's current state of mind is still troubled. Upper and lower loops are compressed revealing repression. Close spacing of words show her need for closeness. A variety of T bars signify continued conflicts. (Plans to rebuild their family home are yet to be finalized.) Signs of humor and rising baselines show her struggle to make light of an otherwise miserable situation.

CASE HISTORY #3:
Mary Alice Dohm

Alice was reared in a disciplined religious environment where high ideals were instilled in her at an early age. She was always a little shy but expressed herself musically by playing the piano.

For most of her adult life she worked as a secretary, with exceptional skills in computers and accounting. Her ability to work in a routine manner made her an asset to any employer. She was a perfectionist who always needed her surroundings in good order.

Over the years, she grew increasingly dissatisfied with the lack of purpose in her life. A desire to help others and a strong need to develop more spiritual harmony prompted Alice to become a nun.

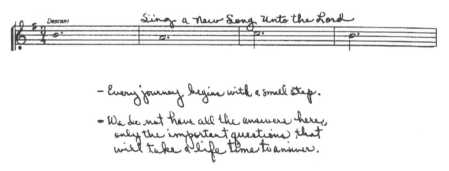

Mary Alice - While living in a convent.

This sample of handwriting was written some time after entering a convent. Notice the left slant, small size, light pen pressure and very close word spacing. This combination of factors indicates her spiritual interests and "retreat" from the outside world. Round formations, connected letters, and even margins displays her conformity to a set pattern of existence.

Wide lower loops and the small printed s reveal her musical talent, which she expressed in daily services. Her carefully controlled rhythm and disciplined T bars indicate a methodical lifestyle in a somewhat restricted environment.

Due to a number of family problems, Alice left the order and returned to the chaos of the real world.

Now I spend my Sundays as a religion teacher for pre-schoolers (which is certainly a challenge) and also as a Eucharistic minister during Mass. I am also a volunteer for one of the local Crisis Pregnancy agencies. It is a great blessing to be of service for Our Lord once again.

Mary Alice Dohn

Mary Alice - After leaving the convent.

Most noticeably different is the size of her handwriting. Her life of seclusion has become more socially oriented. She has reentered the work force . Her medium pen pressure and extended final on the end of her signature shows a greater interest in people, although she still prefers the peacefulness of quiet solitude. To satisfy her spiritual needs, she serves as a Eucharistic minister and is involved in a number of volunteer activities.

CASE HISTORY # 4: J.L.

In the course of a lifetime, a human being undergoes many evolutionary changes. Various factors play significant roles in his developing personality. At the moment of conception, his temperament is predetermined, as well as many other genetic characteristics, depending upon the family into which he is born.

In early years, outside influences such as parents, family members, teachers, and friends shape his pliable nature. His attitudes form early and may last a lifetime. As the young adult personality emerges, the arena of outside influences widens to include additional personal and intimate relationships.

His choices along the journey very much depend upon his success or failure over a period of time. If the choices he makes do not fulfill his needs or ideals, he eventually makes new choices which lead in a different direction. New people, environmental locale, education, and assorted perspectives add depth to the broadening character.

Viewing the evolutionary growth of a developing personality through his handwriting is most insightful. In early years, roundness of letters, connected writing, and initial strokes are all consistent in the immature writer. As the personality develops, and outside influences make lasting impressions, his handwriting will reflect his growing maturity.

A very interesting case is J.L., who at a young age become a Protestant minister. After five years of disillusionment (both personal and religious), he decided to leave the ministry. An avid writer, poet and philosopher, J.L. wrote this penetrating aphorism around the time of his departure from the church.

We must be aware that everything that we say should at least be heard by ourselves.!

J.L. - Age 25.

Most outstanding in his writing are downslant T bars, upper compressed loops, and falling baselines. At this point he was expressing frustration, hopelessness, and a desire to control his own destiny. Light pen pressure denotes spiritual concerns. Notice the round letters and connected writing, depicting his childlike emotions and obedience to set rules. The T bars take on a defiant look, revealing his determination to break from conformity and alter his way of life.

My hands are curled like his, you say, but don't deceive yourself. I can open them if I try.

J.L - Age 45.

A strong quality of independent thought engulfs this sample of handwriting at age forty-five. J.L. continued his education, became an architect, and remarried. Ardent sensuality and emotional expressions are seen in his heavy pen pressure and right slant. His youthful idealism has been transformed into a more realistic lifestyle. His creative intellect is quickly scrawled across the page with short stops of intuitive flashes. Talent and versatility (small printed s) coupled with a strong driving force reveals productive expressions.

With the elimination of many upper and lower loops he has learned to think clearly without unnecessary details. The altruistic y (lines one and two), open small a, and extended finals, disclose profuse generosity. Rising baselines show enthusiasm and optimism. A variety of T bars invade his script, some displaying an adventurous spirit, and others showing a lighter side of his serious nature. The overall picture of his character at this point is one of confident independence and creative expression.

In those lonely hours when sleep my
soul doth flee

Let this upon my stone be penned
and placed for all to see.

Here lies one who could have
been, but for time was never to be.

J.L - Age 60.

At this stage in his life, he openly expresses feelings of futility in the grand scheme of things. He is under constant pressure with heavy workloads. His frustrations are evidenced by erratic baselines which temporarily rise and fall. Perfectionism (even margins and high T bars in second line "doth") and controlling attitudes (downslant T bars and angular letter connections) are evident. He can be inflexible, especially if he believes he is right, and argues any point with conviction. He has become extremely analytical. The extended final in his signature, which is omitted here, corroborates his continued need to give to others. At the present time, he is looking forward to retirement. He hopes to finish a book he is writing on American politics.

Chapter 6

Career Choices

When trying to determine an individual's vocational aptitudes the use of handwriting analysis can be most revealing. The writer's extroverted or introverted personality traits play a major role in his choice of career.

Most writers fall into the category of the extrovert; his energies flow towards other people. Emotionally demonstrative, his feelings lead him into a vocation which offers social interaction. His handwriting slants to the right, is medium to large in size, and possesses medium to heavy pen pressure (depending upon his physical nature). Nursing, teaching, welfare work, law and the ministry are included in this social-oriented area. An analytical ability (connected writing plus sharp m's and n's) is a key attribute in law related careers. Spiritual indications (lighter pen pressure plus the T bar, bowed above the stem) are usually evident in the writing of the clergy.

Large to extra large handwriting, right slanting, and containing long rhythmic lower loops, heavy pen pressure, and down slant T bars reveals the aggressive extrovert who is typically the sales type. He is a dynamo, wheeling and dealing. If his writing is strongly confident and displays good organizational skills (large capitals, average spacing and even margins) he will show an aptitude for management.

The writer who chooses a conventional vocation usually possesses a practical approach to life. He enjoys working in a routine environment. The size of his handwriting expresses the extent of his social interaction. This vast category includes office and secretarial work, research, computer related jobs, and some areas of accounting. The conventional handwriting may contain a vertical to right slant, medium size script, connected writing, medium pen pressure, and middle zone focus. Signs of good judgment, self-discipline, and math ability are also common attributes.

Any writer who possesses small to microscopic handwriting is an introvert, whose energies are inwardly absorbed. His mental intellect governs his choice of career, and he prefers working alone. His strong ability to concentrate gives him a definite aptitude for a specialized vocation. Science, engineering and other occupations requiring mental focus, fall into this area.

Handwriting which reveals self-expressing characteristics belong to the artist, writer, or creative personality. Signs of originality, intuitive perception, creative intellect, and talent will be seen in his script. The freedom to express his own creativity is a paramount factor in the choice of his vocation, and he will more than often forego monetary compensations for the sheer fulfillment of his expressive nature.

The person who chooses a self-employed route is bound to show strong independence in his handwriting. His script will not only contain large capital letters, but many confident capital I's as well. Some form of aggressiveness or need to control will surface, as well as a spirit of adventure. He will often be stubborn and persistent. His determination to excel in his own individuality is a driving force in his personality makeup. The writer is usually quite versatile and easily adapts to the demands of an unconventional lifestyle.

Good judgment will hopefully appear in his writing as well as other positive traits that will enable him to succeed in his endeavors. Depending upon the type of business the entrepreneur chooses, the size of his handwriting will vary.

In this chapter, you will find a smattering of the wide variety of career choices as well as their accompanying personality traits. Each handwriting sample reveals special aptitudes for the writer's chosen vocation. As a general rule, the larger the writing, the greater the aptitude for social-oriented vocations, the smaller the writing, the greater the aptitude for specialized work.

NURSE   Colleen Hess

Colleen's gracious handwriting is an amiable extension of her warmhearted, sentimental nature. She is openly sympathetic, and possesses a compassionate spirit. Her childlike emotions reflect strong dependency ties. An obvious "angel of mercy," she is greatly concerned with the welfare of other people. She is guilty of spreading herself too thin in an effort to accommodate others. Her busy life appears crowded and full of overlapping situations. This causes her some frustration, but you would hardly suspect as much. A person of strong stamina and persistent nature, she is completely dedicated to all those within her reach. (Colleen is a registered nurse who specializes in pediatrics. She has recently taken a leave of absence from her career to devote more time to her family. Her caring disposition creates an aura of loving kindness to everyone she meets.)

It is such a wonderful reflection of ourselves and who we are. Thank you for doing this book and best of luck to you!

Colleen Hess

Major Emphasis: Heavy pen pressure, right slant, large size, legible/round letters, firmly centered/high/star-shaped/tent-like/single stroke/T bars, no margins, initial strokes, large capitals, connected writing, even base line, tangling/lower zone, compressed upper loops.

PUBLIC RELATIONS   Kathy Henscheid

This young woman typifies the exhibitionist who enjoys doing things in a big way. A childlike enthusiasm, generous spirit, and affable disposition reveals her social oriented aptitude for public relations work. An overpowering need for order and harmony is paramount in her handwriting, which reveals her perfectionism. She is a natural organizer. Consistent signs all point to her need for control in whatever she attempts. A logical thinker and clever strategist, she is able to subtly maneuver others to her point of view. Independent, confident, and persistent, she manages to reach desired goals one way or another! The final letter enclosure on "Kathleen" reveals a protective side to her nature, prompting her to reflect on past experiences. (Kathy has been working in public relations for several years and enjoys the people contact. Her enthusiasm and fun-loving approach to life is contagious to everyone around her. A compulsive organizer, she admits to needing strict order and control of her work as well as home environment.)

I wish that everyone could be as lucky as I am!
Kathleen Henscheid

Major Emphasis: Medium pen pressure, right slant, very large size, T bars/looped, firm, exact i dots, balanced zones, controlled rhythm, frequent initial strokes, extended final strokes, very large capital letters, framed margins, wide letter, word and line spacing, legible/connected writing, high mound/small m, strategist capital H, signature/final stroke enclosed.

REPORTER/WRITER Maria Eftimiades

The presence of conflicting signs and crowded margins reveals Maria's busy agenda. No doubt she is being pulled in many directions. Fortunately, she is quite flexible and adapts easily to change. She aggressively pursues goals. Sound judgment coupled with strong intuitive faculties enables her to quickly gauge the heart of a situation. She is able to remain objective while her pragmatic, analytical mind picks up essential facts along the way. A strong, independent attitude and a need for control are evident. Her large signature indicates her desire to make a good impression, though she has a tendency to underestimate herself. (Maria is a talented reporter/writer for People Magazine and is a published author. Traveling extensively to keep abreast of the current news stories, she maintains a rather hectic lifestyle.)

Dear Judy,

I'm very flattered you thought to include me in your book.

Maria Eftimiades

Major Emphasis: Medium/varying pen pressure, varying slant, large size, varying T bars/downslant T bars, tent-like/wavy/exact/to right i dots, small capitals (including small capital I), large unusual/embellished capital M in signature, higher second mound, underscored signature, single upper/lower downstrokes, middle zone focus, blunt endings, sharp points on m's and n's, closed small b, open small a, closed small o, connected/disconnected wiring, no margins, angular lower loops, wide spacing between letters/words/lines, upper compressed loops, altruistic y and g, printscript, vacillating baseline.

ORTHODONTIST   Joe Ainsworth

A consistent, well-balanced handwriting mirrors the image of
Dr. Ainsworth's basic nature. On all levels, he is very organized and
quite the perfectionist. His strong powers of concentration, analytical mind, and attention to detail are obvious assets in his profession.
Steady hand control and self-discipline are solid attributes. He is firmly
independent and can be stubborn in his convictions. A blend of good
judgment, intuition, and business sense are incorporated throughout
his writing. Strong introverted qualities express his need to spend
some time apart from others. He is a thinker as well as a doer. Love
of the outdoors and physical activity are revealed. He is a very sensitive, caring and extremely generous person. Well-adjusted, dedicated,
cheerful and optimistic, he seems to have all the positive characteristics that a successful individual requires (Dr. Ainsworth has been practicing orthodontics for twenty-three years. He is also an avid sports-
man who enjoys bird hunting, but his real passion in life is fishing)

She adds so much to our
office, great people skills, warm beautiful
smile, sense of humor and true dedication
to our office team!   Joe Ainsworth

Major Emphasis: Medium pen pressure, right slant, medium/
small size, bowed/downslant/centered T bars, careful punctuation,
wavy i dots, angular/sharp points, even rhythm, large capitals, open
capital A, closed capital D, looped small d, closed small b, occasional
initial stroke/extended end strokes, good line/word spacing, framed
margins, wide upper loops, connected writing, occasional disconnected
writing, elimination of loop on downstroke letter f, positive signa-
ture/rising base line.

BUSINESS CONSULTANT   Ellen Magnis

Ellen's quick handwriting illustrates the pace of her keen intellect. She is a pragmatist, pure and simple. Stripping down to "just the facts," she is able to reach logical conclusions in a minimum of time. A combination of analytical ability, intuitive awareness and consistent good judgment allows her to instinctively size up situations accurately. Keeping some distance between herself and others allows her an objective perspective. Diplomatic and tactful, she does not invite confrontation, but will stand her ground if sufficiently provoked. She is extremely versatile and easily adapts to changing situations. A person of simple tastes, she also shows a strong appreciation for art and literature. Ambitious and disciplined, this bright young woman has all the positive attributes of the independent entrepreneur. (Ellen is self-employed. As a business consultant, her company, Magnis Communications, offers professional support for physicians. This includes assistance with lectures, journal articles, and setting up new practices. She also assists in resolving conflicts between partners when dissolving medical practices.)

> You can pick out what
> you want — That way
> you won't have to return
> anything!   Love —
>   Ellen

Major Emphasis: Medium pen pressure, vertical slant, medium size, firmly centered/high rising/single stem/T bars, quick rhythm/speed, even/rising base line, printscript, disconnected/connected writing, simple capitals, single stroke small i, elimination upper loops, angular m's, abrupt/rising finals, wide word/line spacing, framed margins, signature/same/tapering letters.

SOCIAL WORKER   Jackie Brown

Jackie's handwriting expresses her overwhelming need to put the well-being of others before her own. A spiritual quality embraces her script which indicates a strong religious background. Emotional ties to the past are evident. Her idealistic, selfless temperament is very sympathetic, patient, and understanding. Aggressive signs reveal her ability to take on challenges. She possesses good organizational skills, is very logical, practical, and prefers a regimented routine in her surroundings. (Jackie is a full-time volunteer for the Mental Health and Mental Retardation Agency. She manages a training workshop/thrift store for MHMR workers. Her duties include supervising employees and organizing the resale of donated merchandise. A steady guiding influence and a person of deep religious conviction, she serves in an unselfish endeavor to improve the lives of those less fortunate.)

We discovered we have three new kittens but still waiting for two more litters. The dog with one baby is doing well but the other pair is still courting, oh well.

Jacqueline Brown

Major Emphasis: Medium pen pressure, right slant, medium size, rigid base line, connected writing, initial strokes, T bar bowed above stem, downslant T bars, wavy i dots, rising finals, careful punctuation, large capitals/upper zone reach, even margins, close word spacing.

JUDGE   Ed Kinkead

Strong reasoning powers and good common sense dominate Ed's handwriting. His analytical mind is quick to form logical decisions. He is a confident, straightforward, open and honest individual. A traditional thinker, he is most comfortable with conventional rules. He will aggressively argue a point if he feels he is in the right and can be quite stubborn. His nature is warm and compassionate. Extreme family pride and strong dependency ties engulf his script. In this particular sample, signs of stress appear now and then, more than likely a result of "too many irons in the fire." Not a big deal for this energetic fellow. He's certain to chalk it up as another challenge. A genuine fun-loving attitude and a good sense of humor enables him to approach life with youthful enthusiasm and real gusto. (Ed is a Justice in the Court of Appeals in Dallas, Texas. During the O.J. Simpson trial, he delivered a daily commentary on a Dallas television program.)

Well, I'm the luckiest guy around.

Ed Kinkead

Major Emphasis: Heavy pen pressure, right slant, large size, firmly entered/wavy/downslant/tent-like T bars, wavy/tent-like i dots, large capitals, round/legible formations, angular/sharp tops and points, connected writing, uneven margins, good line spacing, close word spacing, initial strokes, rising/extended finals, letter corrections, erratic base line/rhythm, wide upper loops, signature/positive/incurve capital K.

SALES   Janette Smith

This self-starter's handwriting refuses to stay on an even baseline. She is the incurable optimist! Her script contains all the necessary attributes of the productive entrepreneur. She is independent, confident, and has a good business sense. Sound practical judgment is clearly evident. Her self-imposed goals are often too demanding, but she is able to overcome most obstacles with strong determination. Though she has a high energy level, her writing reveals some frustration and stress. Extreme family pride and strong ties to the past are indicated. She is openhearted, sensitive, and very emotional. Her fun-loving sense of humor is one of her greatest assets. (Janette and her husband have owned and operated a tractor/sales business for twenty-six years. In addition, Janette is an independent antique dealer. She also has two grown children and a sixteen year old son who keeps her active. This steadfast, energetic woman certainly deserves a much needed vacation from her crowded lifestyle.)

Major Emphasis: Heavy pen pressure, right slant, large size, variety/T bars, wavy i dots, large capitals/including confident capital I, small closed letter b, small looped letter d, connected writing, occasional initial strokes, rising end strokes, compressed upper/lower loops, angular formations, no margins, letter corrections, careful line spacing, tapering letters, elimination of loops, rising base line, incurve capital J, narrow letter spacing/signature.

BUILDING CONTRACTOR   Dick Maddox

Dick's design printing is aesthetically pleasing to the graphological eye. His strong feelings for order and harmony are quite apparent. He is not only highly artistic but possesses a distinct capacity for creating some very original ideas. He is well-organized and very much the perfectionist. Hard driving and intent on desired goals, he often incurs feelings of frustration. A need for control is indicated, for he is extremely independent and self-motivated. His nature is very reserved and cautious. Secretiveness is evident in his signature, for he prefers to keep some things to himself. (Dick is a highly-creative self-employed contractor. He has been in business for fifteen years. His college major was advertising design.)

> I AM WRITING THIS PARAGRAPH AT THE REQUEST OF THE AUTHOR OF THIS BOOK AS A SAMPLE OF MY STYLE OF PENMANSHIP.
>
> Dick Maddox

Major Emphasis: Very heavy pen pressure/shaded strokes, vertical slant, very large size, high rising/hooks/T bars, i dot/left-tending/signature, all caps/design/printing, capital M/second higher mound, even margins, wide word spacing, large capitals, enclosed letters within capital D/signature, extended final/small k/signature, blunt ending stroke/capital M/signature, unusual small letters d/signature.

PARALEGAL   Kathy McWilliams

Logic prevails in this entirely connected handwriting. Kathy prefers a routine or conventional work approach. Well organized and analytical, she also has a keen eye for detail. She enjoys some social contact in her job but is capable of working alone. A good sense of humor prevails throughout her script. Agreeable, kind and enthusiastic, she embraces the qualities of the dependable, reliable employee. (Kathy works as a paralegal in Dallas, Texas. She is married and the mother of two children.)

The sky was blue and the grass grew & grew. Too bad because the lawn mower was broken -- living in the goats.

Kathy McWilliams

Major Emphasis: Medium pen pressure, right slant, medium size, firmly crossed T bars, wavy/tent-like i dots, legible/round letters, initial strokes, rising finals, connected writing, middle zone focus, even base line, steady rhythm, even margins, compressed upper loops, even word spacing sharp m's/n's, signature/same.

TEACHER   Gloria Phillips

Gloria's handwriting reflects the harmonious attributes of the natural-born educator. Self-disciplined and patient, she also feels a need to contribute something worthwhile to others. She is very sensible and well-organized. A lighthearted, altruistic person, she is quick to offer a sympathetic word and she approaches life with unwavering enthusiasm. (After forty-two years of teaching home economics, Gloria recently retired. She is one of those rare teachers whose positive influence has created a lasting impression in the lives of her students. At the present time she is enjoying her role as a grandmother.)

I'll be thinking of you with your knee surgery! Stay happy and remember I love you!

Gloria

Major Emphasis: Medium pen pressure, right slant, medium size, legible/round letter formations, occasional initial stroke, firmly centered T bars, tent-like/high i dots, steady base line, even rhythm,

SURVEYOR   Jack Schoppa

Small, modest handwriting reveals a specialized aptitude for Jack's career in surveying. Basically an introvert, he prefers to work independently in an isolated environment. Good powers of concentration, organizational skills, an exacting eye for detail and a keen critical sense add to his proficiency. Consistent signs of logic, math ability and good judgment are also strong assets. He is an intensely emotional person but does not readily express his feelings. Unassuming and easygoing, he often underestimates his own capabilities. Erratic signs reveal unsettling directions and stress. (Jack is a self-employed surveyor as well as a former teacher.)

Major Emphasis: Medium pen pressure, slight right varying slant, small size, variety T bars/center bowed, exact/tent-like/wavy/i dots, small/printed/capitals, small looped d, small closed lip b, single downstrokes, middle zone focus, wide line spacing, erratic word spacing, wide letter spacing, inconsistent letter size, threaded connections.

DIVERSIFIED ENTREPRENEUR   Phil Knapp

Independence governs this handwriting from the outset, with printed script. A spirit of adventure combined with tenacious determination drives him to pursue a variety of interests. Phil has a sensible, practical nature and a strong sense of economy. Unique-looking capitals express his capacity for original ideas. He has the ability to sublimate strong passions as well as paternal instincts into productive goals. Self-sufficient and self-motivated, he prefers doing things his own way. There is a need for control in his script (a common trait in the entrepreneur). Letter inconsistencies and hooks on T bars reveal nervous energy and restlessness. Humor and generosity are positive attributes. His signature reveals a number of things: excellent powers of concentration, pragmatic thinking, logic as well as intuition, and a desire for privacy. (Phil and his wife recently fulfilled a lifelong dream by moving from Texas to Alaska, where he is involved in a diversity of projects.)

Major Emphasis: Medium/shaded pen pressure, slight right slant, medium size/all caps printing, consistent bowed/T bars and wavy/high/T bars/ hooks, capital M/higher second mound, independent/single stroke/ capital I formations, streamlined version/ old-fashioned capital N "needed" final line, initial stroke/capital A, middle zone focus, inconsistent letter size, signature: illegible/small size/reverse capital P/ unusual capital F/single and retraced strokes/ omission of punctuation, no margins.

> WE ARE TRYING TO START A AQUA-CULTURE HYDROPONICS GREEN HOUSE TO RAISE ORGANIC VEGGIES AND HERBS, BUT THE SYSTEM NEEDS FISH AND FISH FARMING IN ALASKA IS PROHIBITED AT THIS TIME, MOSTLY FROM FEAR OF DISEASE AND NON-NATIVE FISH IN AREA WATERS. WE ARE TRYING TO GET A SPECIAL PERMIT FOR IMPORT OF THE WARM WATER FISH NEEDED.

Chapter 7

The Intimate Relationship: Compatibility

In the past forty years, the concept of marriage in the United States has acquired a whole new perspective. Today one out of two marriages ends in divorce. Not long ago, couples married with dreams of having an ideal family. "A boy for you, and a girl for me," was a typical American standard. But today, the phrase "extended family" has become an accepted norm in a large number of households. Couples raising children from previous marriages deal with the hassle of child-support, visitation schedules, and a variety of accompanying emotional problems.

It has become almost a rarity these days when a couple manages to celebrate 25, much less 50 years of wedded bliss. So just what does constitute the success of a long-term relationship? Many couples cite trust, intimacy, and mutual respect as the foundation for their longevity together. Their marital accord may also be partially attributed to the personality traits of the particular individuals involved. One couple might be more willing to accept the same problems another couple would not possibly tolerate. Just as there are no absolute answers for successful relationships, there are just as many reasons why marriages fail. These range from sheer boredom to more serious problems including mistrust, abusive conduct and infidelity.

Psychologists and marriage counselors find graphology to be an invaluable tool. Hidden traits disclosed in a couple's handwriting often provides helpful insight into troubled relationships. In searching for mutual signs of compatibility in a couple's writing, the first thing to consider is what types of personalities are involved. Are they both extroverts, introverts, or a combination of the two? Do they also share common goals, similar ways of thinking or similar outlooks?

In addition, other important factors to take into consideration are: sexual compatibility, tolerance, generosity, and a good sense of humor. You might think that sexual compatibility is the most important element to consider. Yet many couples marry in the heat of desire only to discover that once the passion cools, they have little, if anything, left in common. After a period of time, many couples place lesser interest in sexual concerns, and often rechannel their sexual energy into other areas of mutual interest. (See page 39 for indications.)

Couples whose handwritings show signs of tolerance and generosity will also have a greater chance of creating a more harmonious and lasting relationship. Gentle, round formations and extended finals are positive indications. Excessive behavior, including intolerant attitudes or demands are obvious detriments to a strong, healthy marriage. (See Warning signs, page 59).

In the long run, most individuals require room for personal growth and development in their intimate relationships. Kahil Gibran wrote, "But let there be spaces in your togetherness, and let the winds of the heavens dance between you." Perhaps the most successful marriages are ones in which each individual supports the separate identity of the other.

Regardless of the wide variety of marital perspectives, the addition of humor to any relationship is a most necessary ingredient. Wavy T bars and i dots in a couple's handwriting points to the couple's ability to laugh at their problems along the road to mutual harmony.

The following samples of handwriting belong to a couple who has been married for forty-three years. They are retired.

We enjoyed our trip to Las Vegas but we were glad to get back home

Cloice Johnson

◆◆◆◆◆◆◆

To us was born 7 wonderful Children four boys, And Three girls. And now we Are blessed with 17 grandchildren

Robbie Johnson

Considering this couple has been married for forty-three years, you would automatically assume they must be compatible. Their handwritings certainly reveal tolerance and generosity. They are both extroverted personalities who share common interests. Each reveals strong dependency ties. Cloice possesses steady self-control and an exacting eye for detail. He's a logical, practical thinker who approaches everything in an efficient, methodical manner. Robbie is also very logical, but she is intuitive, as well. She is warm, spontaneous and enthusiastic. She does not always finish what she starts and is moody, now and then. Overcrowding her life with a variety of interests often causes a little chaos and disorder. Extreme family pride is quite apparent. Robbie can be abrupt, and openly speaks her mind. Cloice likes to have the final word in an argument (because he insists, he's always right). Both have fun-loving natures, and their laughter keeps their marriage "young at heart."

(Robbie and Cloice enjoy fishing and going to flea markets together. Though Robbie has many interests of her own, she also shares her husband's affection for collecting old time pieces.)

At the far end of the spectrum is a couple who is newly married.

My NAME IS CHRIS BRYANT! ON
JUNE 3rd 1995 I MARRIED RENEE
BURKHART. I AM A 23 year OLD
SALES REP. I Enjoy water SKiing and
Customizing PiCK-UP TRUCKS! I AM
PRESENTly Living In the StatE of
OKlahoma!

                    ChriS Bryant

◆◆◆◆◆◆◆

My name is Renee Bryant. I am 25 years
old. I recently got married to Chris Bryant.

These newlyweds have only been together two months. Chris
has many of the usual elements of the sales personality. He has youthful
enthusiasm, is hard driving and ambitious. Signs of stress are apparent in his writing. He is independent, impulsive, and quick to express
his opinions. Renee's personality is gentle and protective. She is friendly
but reserved and exhibits good self-confidence. Her entire writing
expresses her sensible thinking. She does not have the driving force
her new husband displays, but she can be persistent, when needed.
Of the two personalities, she is obviously the more steadying influence in the relationship. Their energies are focused in realistic directions. While he is busy pursuing new projects, she will be diligently
building her own business in the beauty field. These two indepen-
dents will surely disagree at times, but they seem to share the drive
and ambition to reach common goals. There are enough harmonious
traits in their writing to indicate their willingness to make necessary
adjustments. At the very least, their life together should not be dull.

The following couple has been together for thirteen years. They
were high school sweethearts. They have three little girls.

*required me to stop + think I found it actually
form the letters. Quite an experience.*

◆◆◆◆◆◆◆

*Glenn and J met in 1982. We were
married in 1988. Who would have
Vickie Fisher*

Vickie's personality is gentle, sympathetic and patient. Easygoing and
flexible, she quickly adapts to new circumstances. Though appearing
friendly, she is somewhat reserved and is able to remain objective
while forming opinions. She is confident, independent and practical.
Good organizational skills are apparent as well as a keen eye for detail. Glenn's printing and illegible signature reveals his introverted
nature. Behind his public image, however, lies a warm, caring personality. He appears to be something of a mystery to others, and he
prefers it that way. Initial strokes coupled with left tending formations reveal strong ties to the past, while the outward appearance
aspires more towards the future. Both handwritings contain introverted and extroverted characteristics as well as strong dependency
ties. Basically gentle and compassionate by nature, they each possess
the agreeable traits for a sustained relationship. (Glenn is an electri-
cal engineer. His printed script is symptomatic of his profession. Vickie
is a CPA/Operating Accountant for the Federal Government. They
also volunteer for Engaged Encounter.)

Strong personalities are indicated in the following samples of this couples' handwriting.

Between the boys and my work schedule I stay very busy. Any free time might be spent on the golf course.

would tell you my hobbies, but who has time for those?

Danna Fredrick

John and Danna are the parents of four small sons. Both have high energy levels and confident personalities. John is a zealous, intensely emotional person. Strong executive attributes including independence, foresight, persistence, good judgment and business sense are all outstanding in his writing. His signature reveals his desire to make a good impression. The enclosed letters indicate secretiveness and reveal a more reclusive public image. Behind the exterior facade lies a warm, congenial good-natured personality. Danna is a spontaneous extrovert, open, honest, sympathetic and patient. She has an active agenda (no margins), and all the complementary characteristics necessary for a career in teaching or parenting. Both writings reveal compatible traits including tolerance, generosity and a good sense of humor. (Danna is a former elementary teacher. John is General Manager of Fredrick Management Corporation.)

The following samples of writing belong to a couple who is struggling with difficult circumstances.

Meet me at Denny's for breakfast in the morning.

◆◆◆◆◆◆◆

so glad that he made it to the party Sat. night, & he had a good time!

Barbara and Al have been married for eighteen years. They both have children from first marriages. Barbara had low self-esteem when she first met Al and was attracted to his take-charge forcefulness. Al loved the idea of having someone he could control. Over the years, Barbara has grown increasingly unhappy but does not have the willpower to start a new life again on her own. With the children grown and gone, living alone together has not improved this couple's marriage. To add to the stress, Al is convinced he has not been able to find work due to his age. He has developed an intolerant attitude towards everyone, including his wife. Sexual problems have added to this already strained relationship. Barbara's sensitive temperament has all but collapsed under the pressure. Her kind, passive nature is no match for the domineering behavior expressed by her husband. Hopefully with counseling, they will be able to come to terms with their difficulties.

Many couples form lifetime commitments without seeming to share any mutual interests. Their complacency often forms a secure pattern in their lives together. The following couple is such an example.

if you feel like you want to talk call me collect. Anyway

◆◆◆◆◆◆◆

When I could say or do something to help.

This couple has been married over thirty years. David is a warm, honest person with strong dependency ties. His existence is rather routine. He has grown accustomed to living in quiet desperation with his wife, Estelle. She is almost a hermit. She seldom leaves the security of her home and is adamant about keeping everything in order, including David. His feelings of frustration cause him to rebel occasionally, and he has developed a drinking problem. His need for more social contact often drives him to seek companionship with others but after awhile, he returns to her isolated world for their common bond is their mutual dependency.

Chapter 8

Changing Personality Through Handwriting

Do you ever wish you could change your own personality? Most of us at one time or another have wanted more self-confidence or stronger willpower to overcome weaker habits. Professional counseling and hypnosis can be most useful and play a large part in this progressive movement toward self-improvement.

A method known as Graphotherapy has been used for many years in Europe and is enjoying new found success in this country as well. Through the power of suggestion, various ideas are "programmed" into specially designed handwriting exercises to promote more positive feelings in the writer.

For instance, the writer who constantly fails to cross a T bar through the stem (𝓣) can be described as a chronic procrastinator. His inability to finish things is due primarily to a fear of failure, more than anything else. Practicing handwriting exercises that produce long, horizontal strokes that firmly cross the T bar (𝓣) will give him a feeling of forging ahead, following through, and completing a task. This surge of action will eventually, if not immediately, be felt by the writer and over a period of time will help alleviate his frustrations in this area.

The less confident writer who often forms small capital letters in his handwriting exhibits low self-esteem. Stronger feelings of confidence could be developed by practicing handwriting exercises focusing on large capitals, including special emphasis on the capital I, and the writer's own signature, as well. The overwhelming feeling of confidence is perhaps the single most important characteristic of a person's total make up and well worth developing, no matter what methodology is used.

Another feeling very common to most people at one time or another is depression. In handwriting this is most noticeable in the downslant of letters or in the drooping of lines. If you suffer severe depression over a long period of time, you should seek professional help, but for an occasional bout of the "blues," a person might try practicing a positive handwriting exercise, writing on an upslant and adding a few high rising end strokes for a little extra enthusiasm.

If this all sounds a bit too simplistic, try looking at the concept from a different perspective. What brightens your outlook when you feel sad or a little depressed? Some people watch a funny movie to relieve the doldrums, go for a long walk, or talk to a sympathetic friend who will listen. The key is to do something that will help to change your depressed mood!

While the ideas expressed here are conceived from my own practical viewpoint, other handwriting exercises for specific changes in personality traits could be uniquely created to suit your particular circumstance.

Practice Exercises

Here are a few suggestions. Every day write (three or four times) the following exercise which best suits your personal needs:

For will power and determination, practice writing long straight T bars. Example:

I am determined to finish this tonight.

I am determined to finish this tonight.

For self-esteem and confidence, practice writing large capitals with emphasis on the capital I and your own signature (see page 34 for your own preference of capital I's). Example:

I am _____ and I am special.

I am Laura Carter and I am special.

For optimism and enthusiasm, practice writing on an upslant with high rising end strokes. Example:

It's a wonderful life!

It's a wonderful life!

Bibliography

Amend, Karen and Mary S. Ruiz. ACHIEVING COMPATIBILITY WITH HANDWRITING ANALYSIS. North Hollywood, CA: Newcastle Publishing Co., Inc. 1992.

Kursden, Stephen. GRAPHOLOGY-THE NEW SCIENCE. Washington, D.C.: Acropolis Books, Ltd. 1971

Kurtz, Sheila, & Lester, Marilyn. GRAPHOTYPES. New York, New York: Crown Publishers, Inc. 1983.

Le Guen, Monique. GRAPHOLOGY. S.A., Nyon: Media Books, 1976.

Mahoney, Ann. HANDWRITING AND PERSONALITY. New York, New York: Henry Holt and Company, Inc. 1989.

Marcuse, Irene. GUIDE TO PERSONALITY THROUGH YOUR HANDWRITING. New York, New York: Arc Books, Inc. 1967.

Olyanova, Nadya. HANDWRITING TELLS. New York, New York: The Bobbs-Merrill Company, Inc. 1969.

Olyanova, Nadya. THE PSYCHOLOGY OF HANDWRITING. North Hollywood, CA: Wilshire Book Company. 1960.

Paterson, Jane. INTERPRETING HANDWRITING. New York: David McKay Company, Inc. 1976.

Roman, Klara G. HANDWRITING A KEY TO PERSONALITY. New York, New York: Pantheon Books, Inc. 1952.

Rosen, Billie Pesin. THE SCIENCE OF HANDWRITING ANALYSIS. New York: Bonanza Books. 1965.

Santoli, Ornella. HOW TO READ HANDWRITING. New York, New York: Crown Publishers Inc. 1988.

Sara, Dorothy. HANDWRITING ANALYSIS FOR THE MILLIONS. New York, New York: Bell Publishing Company Inc. 1967.

Gullan-Whur. THE GRAPHOLOGY WORKBOOK. Wellingborough, Northhamptonshire: The Aquarian Press. 1986.

Soloman, Shirl. KNOWING YOUR CHILD THROUGH HIS HANDWRITING AND DRAWINGS. New York, New York: Crown Publishers, Inc. 1978.

Teltscher, Henry O. HANDWRITING-REVELATION OF SELF. New York: Hawthorn Books, Inc. 1971.

Index

Olyanova, Nadya 9
open letters 36
optimism 47
orthodontist's writing 102

paralegal writing 108
pen pressure 22
period after name 31, 80
personnel work 11
poet 43
printing 44
printscript 44
practice exercises 123
public-relations 100

Richards, Ann 86
rhythm 27

sales 106
scratching, word 59
scribblings 69
self-expressive
    vocations 98, 101
sex, indeterminate 15
sexual interest 39, 113
shaded pen stroke 22
signatures 53
size 25
slant 23
small letters 36
social-oriented
    vocations 97, 99, 100,
    104, 105, 106, 109
social worker 104
spacing 48
specialized vocation 98,
    102, 110

speedy writing 27
surveyor's writing 110

T bars 28
teacher's writing 109

underscored
    signature 54, 101
upper loops 38

warning signs 59
Wayne, John 84
Williams, Robin 55
writer's handwriting 101

Zaslow, Michael 61
zones 26

Order Form

HANDWRITING ANALYSIS
A COMMON SENSE GUIDE

Please send check or money order to:

Judy Inman
P.O. Box 492
Saint Jo, TX 76265-0492

$ 9.95 each
   .72 state tax
  <u>1.50 postage</u>
$12.17 total per book

Dealers prices on request.

Other books by the author:

<u>Portrait of Bulcher</u>

<u>Nana's Fun and Easy Cookbook for Kids</u>